What people are saying about
Love Broke Through:

A valuable piece—a needed book for the times. Tom Stribling's book speaks to us all concerning our responsibilities—to others, to ourselves, and to God. What remains with me is Tom's unflinching honesty about himself, his own choices, and his repentance. It was this honesty and repentance, through God's grace, that saved him from a desperate death. Tom came out of the darkness into the light; he faced himself and knelt before Jesus Christ. I knew Tom in his last days—calm, patient in his suffering, and brave. This book will be jeered at by many, but there are many more who will find their way by reading it—who will find the way Tom found.

—Polly Holliday
actress

Here is a penetrating, provocative, profound look at a devastating threat in American life. Transcending prejudice and closed minds, this is the story of one who endured not simply the disease itself but the indifference, the rejection, the blindness, and the anger of many who profess to be recipients of, and channels for, the love of God in Jesus Christ.

—Richard C. Halverson
Chaplain, U.S. Senate
from the "Foreword"

Love
Broke
Through

A Husband, Father, and
Minister Tells His Own Story

by THOMAS B. STRIBLING
with Verne Becker

Zondervan Books
Zondervan Publishing House
Grand Rapids, Michigan

Love Broke Through
Copyright © 1990 by Verne Becker and the Estate of Tom Stribling

Zondervan Books is an imprint of
The Zondervan Publishing House
1415 Lake Drive, S.E.
Grand Rapids, Michigan 49506

Library of Congress Cataloging-in-Publication Data:

Stribling, Thomas B.
   Love broke through : the true story of Tom Stribling / Thomas B.
Stribling with Verne Becker.
       p.   cm.
     ISBN 0-310-52861-5
     1. Stribling, Thomas B. 2. Clergy—United States—Biography.
3. AIDS (Disease)—Patients—United States—Biography. 4. Church
work with the terminally ill. 5. Church work with gays—United
States. 6. AIDS (Disease)—Religious aspects—Christianity.
7. Aids (Disease)—Patients—Pastoral counseling of. I. Becker,
Verne. II. Title.
BR1725.S836A3   1990   90–34669
                                                          CIP

To protect their privacy, the names of some of the AIDS patients, of Tom's ex-wife, of some of Tom's friends, and of the young woman injured in Tom's car accident have been changed in this book. All other names have been retained.

All Scripture quotations, unless otherwise noted, are taken from the *Holy Bible: New International Version* (North American Edition). Copyright © 1973, 1978, 1984, by the International Bible Society. Used by permission of Zondervan Bible Publishers.

Edited by Mary McCormick
Designed by Louise Bauer

Printed in the United States of America

90 91 92 93 94 95 / LP / 10 9 8 7 6 5 4 3 2 1

*To the men of the New York Fellowship
who, through Christ,
gave me back my masculinity*

FOREWORD

Here is a penetrating, provocative, profound look at a devastating threat in American life. Transcending prejudice and closed minds, this is the story of one who endured not simply the disease itself but the indifference, the rejection, the blindness, and the anger of many who profess to be recipients of, and channels for, the love of God in Jesus Christ.

Tom Stribling came into my office on Capitol Hill a year before he died. I listened to his story with excitement and gratitude to God. He was a "trophy of grace" if I have ever seen one, filled with the compassion of Jesus Christ for those who are experiencing the same blind rejection that he had experienced. Tom devoted himself to bringing the love of God, the salvation and deliverance of Jesus Christ, new life, and liberation to those hurting, abandoned, forsaken ones.

It was a privilege to know Tom Stribling, to sense his commitment to devote his life to extending God's love to those who, far too often, were unthinkingly consigned not only to hell on earth, but to eternal separation from God.

Richard C. Halverson
Chaplain
U.S. Senate
May 1, 1990

INTRODUCTION

In a small, stark hospital room at the New York University Medical Center in Manhattan a man lay dying of AIDS. The disease had ravaged his body so completely that he looked like a heap of bones with waxy, blotchy skin stretched over them. He lay in a semi-fetal position, mainly to keep warm since he had no fat to maintain his body temperature. Posted outside the door was a sign that said in large, bold letters: BIOCHEMICAL HAZARD. Whenever nurses entered the room, they wore rubber gloves. When they left, they tossed the gloves in a special covered bin labeled BIOCHEMICAL WASTE.

The man's name was Bill. A talented singer and actor in his forties, Bill had contracted AIDS within the past year, and was deteriorating rapidly. Polly Holliday, an actress friend of his who was a Christian (Polly portrayed Flo on the TV show "Alice"), had been trying to get Bill to think about God, but with no success. Then she heard about Tom Stribling, an ordained Christian minister who also had AIDS. Formerly an active homosexual, Tom had now dedicated his life to sharing Christ's love with AIDS patients and their families. Polly called him and asked if he'd talk to Bill.

Tom and Polly visited Bill together. Tom, who is six-foot-two, with thinning hair and a beard sporting patches of gray, stood next to the bed. He could have had a commanding presence, except that his deep-set eyes and soft smile betrayed a vulnerable side—a side that had experienced a great deal of pain and a profound sense of joy. There was something about Tom that disarmed people and reached into their souls.

His style was simple, quiet, gentle. He spoke slowly in his naturally deep voice, and his words were few. "Bill," he said, "the reason I am here is that Polly asked me to come. I, too, have AIDS. But I want you to know what a difference it has made in my life to have accepted Christ. It's made it much easier to deal with this disease. I feel as though my life is complete now."

Unlike many advanced AIDS patients who suffer mental lapses, Bill was completely coherent. Politely he said, "Thank you, but I think I'm okay on that score. I've got all that together."

Tom didn't press the faith issue. He simply said he'd stop back in a few days.

"Please do that," Bill said.

When Tom returned, alone this time, there was a visitor in Bill's room. Bill asked the visitor to leave for about fifteen minutes, and then turned to Tom. "I think there is something you and I need to talk about," he said. "Last time you asked me if my life was complete. It's really not. There is something missing, and I think I know what it is. Would you mind praying with me?"

Not knowing exactly what to say, Tom bowed his head and prayed, "Lord, please reveal to Bill what it is you want him to do with his life. Please bring him comfort and release from pain." When he opened his eyes, he saw tears streaming down Bill's face.

Then Bill offered his own prayer. It began as more of a deep groan from within, as if his greatest longing had been buried there all his life and only now was escaping. "Oh, Jesus . . . Oh, Jesus," was all he could say at first. Then, through his tears, he added, "I know I haven't been the man you intended me to be, but when I get out of this hospital I will serve you for the rest of my days."

They were silent for a few moments. Then Tom looked at him and said, "Bill, that was a wonderful prayer. I know God heard that."

"I meant every word of it," he replied.

Two weeks later Bill died in his sleep. But Tom and Polly rejoiced because they knew that he had found peace with himself and with God. Tom had perceived this when he had called on Bill again. And during those last two weeks Bill had told everyone who visited him how meaningful his experience of meeting Christ was.

There was something unique about Tom.

Patty knew it, too. She was one of the very first people Tom visited after beginning his ministry in New York. An intravenous drug user, she had become a Christian years before through the Lamb's Church street ministry led by B.J. Weber. But she'd had a hard time kicking her drug habit. Then she learned she had contracted AIDS because she had shared needles.

B.J. had met with her a couple of times, but before long she had deteriorated steadily and needed to be hospitalized. B.J. asked Tom if he'd visit her in the hospital and deliver a card.

When Tom arrived at the hospital, he found her curled up tightly in a fetal position, eyes closed. He wasn't sure she could hear him, so he bent over and said quietly in her ear, "Patty, I am a friend of B.J. Weber. I'm here because B.J. wanted me to tell you how much he loves you. But even more than that, how much Jesus loves you."

The moment Tom mentioned the name of Jesus, Patty's body relaxed and uncoiled as if the tautness had simply flowed out of her. She was only half-conscious, but she managed to mumble under her breath, "I know."

The next time Tom visited her, she was sitting up while a nurse was attempting to feed her. But she was very near death. She was so frail she couldn't have weighed more than eighty pounds; she had no interest in food, and could hardly speak. As soon as Tom entered the room, she recognized him and simply said, "B.J."

"Yes, that's right. I'm a friend of B.J.'s," Tom said.

Patty proceeded to stare at Tom intently. Rather than break the silence out of nervousness, Tom gazed back into her searching eyes. After a long interval, Patty uttered four short words:

"You're a holy man."

Then she fell silent. Once again Tom didn't know how to respond. He didn't think of himself as being holy; he simply felt thankful for what God had done in his life, and he wanted to share it with others. But at this moment he said nothing. He put his hand on Patty's and stayed for a while longer. Apparently Patty, too, had picked up on whatever it was about him that got through to people. She said nothing more during that visit. Shortly thereafter, she died.

What was extraordinary about Tom?

Roger, an executive with a major New York department store, sensed it. He had lived the gay lifestyle for twenty years without ever saying a word to his parents about his sexual orientation. When he finally developed AIDS, he told them he had cancer. He was too afraid they'd reject him outright if they knew the truth.

But then Tom visited Roger and told him that he himself had had the same fear about his own parents—but when he found the courage to be honest with them, he was overwhelmed by their love and support. Within a matter of weeks Roger had not only told everything to his parents (they, too, were loving and understanding), but he had also asked Christ to come into his life.

Before Roger died, he said, "You know, Tom, one of the things that convinced me I needed to change my own life was what I saw in you. The first time you visited me, you reached out and touched my hand, and in that touch I felt something that told me, 'This man knows something that I want to know, too.' "

What did Tom know? The peace and freedom and power of unconditional love. Tom knew, in the deepest part of himself, what it meant to be totally and uncompromisingly loved—by his family, by the church, by God.

Unfortunately, it took him forty-six years of emotional turmoil to discover that love. Even though at age ten he had dedicated his life to God, had later attended seminary and had become a Methodist minister, he didn't find it. Even though he had married a wonderful woman and fathered a beautiful daughter, he didn't find it. And even though he had left them behind to pursue a promiscuous homosexual lifestyle for twenty years, he didn't find it. Yet this love was there all the time—in his parents, in his sisters and brother, in his daughter.

Not until a tragic and extraordinary sequence of events occurred in Tom's life—beginning with the news that he had AIDS—was he able to face his own emptiness and open his heart. But when he did, the love he had so desperately sought all his life poured in—from his sister, Peggy; his brother, Jerry; his daughter, Libby; his parents, friends, and many others.

Overwhelmed, Tom embraced not only his family again, but he embraced the God of the universe, the ultimate source of love.

His life was never the same.

Since then, Tom has said, "The main contribution I think I've made to others is to be a witness to that love. I know that many people I've visited have seen it; they realize that something is different. I only hope that some of those people will finally say, 'I want that love for myself.' "

This is a true story about a lot of things—about homosexuality, AIDS, job discrimination, blackmail, the criminal court system, the church, and family relationships. But most of all it is the story of a man broken and transformed by love.

Love
Broke
Through

*T*he reason New Year's Eve depresses us might possibly be twofold. First, it is because we are reminded that the past year is a closed book. It is water under the bridge that can never be reclaimed. . . .

A second reason we are depressed by New Year's Eve is that it is a reminder that time is running out. It stands like a bad omen calling out the inevitability that death will come to each and every one of us. It reminds, as each new birthday reminds, that death is a year closer. No one likes to be reminded that life is not his for keeps. No one likes to be reminded he will not live forever. . . .

Unfortunately, the attempt to escape these two depressing thoughts by making merry on New Year's Eve does not work. . . . We may party hard, but on the morning after rings the inevitable reminder that the problems we sought to escape are still very much with us. . . . The momentary excursions and diversions we take in the course of an unhappy life are only temporary. They offer no guarantee of longlasting happiness. They are noble but frail attempts to be happy. But real happiness is possible only when we are at peace with ourselves. . . .

As we stand at the threshold of a new year, may we put aside our fears and anxieties. May we be comforted by the good news that God loves us in spite of the past. And that in Christ all things are made new. . . .

From "A New Beginning," a sermon Tom preached for New Year's, 1967

ONE
ONE
ONE
ONE
ONE

It's a warm day in May 1989. I've opened the window of my fifth-floor apartment above the Lamb's Church to let in a little of New York City's stale air, and a lot of its noise. Besides the usual buzzing and blaring of cars, the grunting of delivery trucks, the wailing of sirens, and whistling of miscued auto alarms, my block has been invaded by clattering jackhammers and other heavy equipment. Major construction is going on across the street. I turn up the ringer volume on my phone.

I'm located on 44th Street, one block west of Times Square in the heart of the theater district. This week the marquees herald dramatic appearances by the "Phantom of the Opera," "A Chorus Line," a horde of singing Cats, Sylvester Stallone, Freddy Krueger, and Batman. During the day, dozens of yellow taxis and thousands of commuters clog the square.

The Lamb's Church has generously allowed me and my cat, Adam, to live here rent-free. I feel very taken care of by this community of Christians. Yesterday the church secretary, who lives upstairs, brought down dinner. And a few minutes ago Brad stopped in with a couple of bags of groceries he had picked up for me. (I forgot to put cat food on my grocery list—Adam will have to eat scraps until tomorrow.) Other good friends from the church pop in to say hello and keep me company.

In addition, my family stays in close touch. My parents and my sister Peggy call me (or I call them) nearly every day. I also talk to my brother Jerry and my daughter Libby several times each week.

This morning I got up at 6:30, and followed my usual routine of devoting an hour to Bible reading, meditation, and prayer. Normally I would then scramble an egg or have a bowl of cereal, but I haven't been feeling very hungry lately.

Actually, I haven't been feeling well at all. Last month I spent seven days in the hospital with a fever, loss of appetite, and severe diarrhea. The doctors ran all sorts of tests, but couldn't find any specific cause. My fever eventually disappeared, the diarrhea stopped, and some of my appetite returned, so they sent me home. But I feel myself getting progressively weaker.

I'm moving into the advanced stages of AIDS.

A few days ago the doctor ran a few more tests; he thought he had found something out of the ordinary in my blood. Typically it would indicate the presence of pneumocystis carinii pneumonia, but a chest X-ray showed that my lungs were completely clear. The other possible diagnosis, my doctor told me, was cancer. A galleon scan would tell him for sure. Today he is supposed to call me with the results.

My feelings at the moment are mixed. I feel sad and frustrated that this disease is sapping the life out of me; yet on the other hand, I feel happier than I've been in my entire life. I'm afraid as I think of the additional pain and suffering I'll have to endure; yet deep down, my soul is at peace. I am ready to die.

While I wait for the doctor's call, I reflect on the many turns my life has taken—some tragic, some bizarre, some miraculous—and all redeemed by the relentless love of God.

The phone rings. It's not the doctor.

"Hi, Dad. . . . Well, I'm feeling okay, I guess. . . . No, I haven't heard anything yet, but I'll be sure to let you know. . . . How's Mom today? . . . Uh huh. . . . Yeah. . . . Okay, I'll call as soon as I know. . . . Thanks for checking in. . . . I love you, too, Dad. Bye."

I'm sure the doctor will call eventually. In the meantime, I'll begin my story. It's a hard story for me to tell, and I've been told it's a hard story to listen to— especially when it's heard from a purely human perspective. It's also an ugly story in which many innocent people are hurt by my own selfishness, arrogance, and indifference. Believe me, I am not proud of my part in this story.

But if it is viewed not from a human perspective, but from God's perspective, it can be cause for rejoicing. So in spite of all the pain I have caused myself and others, I can tell this story with joy in my heart. I'll begin with the dark day that would change my life forever: the Saturday night after New Year's Day, 1987.

* * *

I pulled up to the toll booth and fumbled for some change. I was drunk, and I had no idea where I was or what time it was, other than nighttime. Struggling to keep my head clear, I tried to count out the proper amount. Suddenly I noticed several police cars pulling up around me. In a moment they had surrounded my blue Cavalier wagon, cutting me off in front and behind. Bright spotlights shone into my face. *What is going on?* I wondered.

A plain-clothes policeman approached my side of the car, and without warning he pulled the door open and yanked me out. His nightstick whirled at me, landing with a *thud* across the bridge of my nose. As I screamed in pain, the cop threw me to the ground and kicked me in the back. "You drunkard!" I heard him yell at me repeatedly. With his foot he shoved my face down into the pavement, grinding dirt and gravel into my skin. I was already tasting blood from my nose.

Still holding me down on the street, another policeman handcuffed me behind my back and read me my rights. All the while I had no idea what I had done or why I was being arrested. I tried to say something to the arresting officer, but because I was just coming out of my stupor, I couldn't form my words. So he threw me—bruised, scraped, and bleeding—into the back of his car and drove me to the precinct station.

Not until we arrived at the station did it occur to anyone to ask me if I knew what I'd done. By this time my head had cleared enough for me to talk, and I said I didn't know what had happened. The precinct captain told me I had been driving while drunk at about 2:40 A.M. I had struck a girl and severed both of her legs.

I couldn't believe what I was hearing. *How could I have done that?* I wondered. *I know I was drinking, but I don't remember hitting anyone. There must be some mistake.* Then it occurred to me: *I must have blacked out for several hours. The last thing I remember was back in Connecticut around dinnertime when I drove to that bar in Bridgeport.* As I began to realize that I could actually have committed a felony—and that I had no memory of it whatsoever—I grew more and more afraid.

Then someone took me before a video camera and asked me to walk on a straight line, turn around, then walk back and face the camera. Mustering every ounce of self-control that I had left in my body, I concentrated on that line and followed it pretty well. Next I was told to touch my nose with my finger. I hesitated because my nose hurt terribly and was still bleeding, but I was able to touch it without difficulty.

For some reason when they asked me to take the breathalizer test, I refused. Even in my foggy state of mind I knew I must have been pretty drunk to have blacked out.

I had never blacked out like that before. I think I feared that I would blow the top off the breathalizer test and that those results would somehow increase the charges against me.

The precinct captain then proceeded to book me on a number of charges: vehicular assault in the first degree, assault in the first degree, reckless endangerment in the first degree, operating a motor vehicle while under the influence of alcohol, and leaving the scene of an accident without reporting it. I knew instantly that these were very serious charges. (New York State had just conducted a major television campaign against drunk driving, and I knew the possibility of a sentence was real.)

After the ordeal of facing the video camera and being booked, the officers accompanied me to the bathroom, where I was allowed to urinate and to wipe the blood off my face. I was too afraid to tell anyone that the arresting cop had clubbed me with his nightstick even though I had no weapon and had not resisted at the time of arrest.

Finally I was ushered from the precinct station to a little, dank holding cell for the rest of the night. Still handcuffed, I was led to a room with a long row of tiny cells, side by side. Except for the iron bars on the front, my cell was completely concrete, dirty, and blackened. All over the walls and the ceiling, former occupants' initials were smudged. Apparently they had taken matches or cigarettes and burned their inscriptions into the walls. Then I noticed that some of these black initials moved. Cockroaches.

To one side of the cell a hard wooden bench was attached to the wall. Next to the head of the bench stood an open toilet with no seat, vile and filthy. It hadn't been cleaned in centuries, and I learned a few minutes later that it didn't flush. The whole place reeked of urine and feces.

The corrections officer removed my handcuffs and locked me in the cell. I still couldn't believe what was happening. I was in jail. I had never been arrested before in my life. *What am I going to do now? How am I going to get out of here?* I fretted, pacing back and forth. Then the thought occurred to me: *A phone call . . . I'm allowed to make a phone call, right?* I waved for a nearby corrections officer to come over.

"I need to make a call," I said.

"Sorry, it's too late," he replied curtly.

"What do you mean it's too late?" I said, puzzled because no one had even yet mentioned to me that I could make a phone call.

"You have to do that before you're booked," the officer said. "You should have told the precinct captain as soon as you came before him that you wanted to make a phone call. Sorry." Then he turned away.

"But . . . but no one told me. . . ."

The officer didn't look back. Obviously, he wasn't going to help me. So I lay down on the wooden bench, listening to the sounds around me and worrying about what would happen to me come daylight. I especially feared what they would do when they found out two more pieces of information about me: that I was gay, and that I had AIDS.

By now it must have been 3:30 or 4:00 A.M. I couldn't see the guys in the cells on each side of me, but I could hear them calling back and forth to each other, "Got a cig? Got a cig?" Then they'd reach through the bars and pass cigarettes back and forth. But a guard came around every once in a while and took the cigarettes away.

One young man's voice rang out above the others. He must have been strung out on something—probably crack. He carried on a loud tirade throughout the night. Because most of his words didn't make sense, I guessed that he was probably hallucinating.

Gradually the other cells filled up, and as more people were brought in they went into already-occupied cells.

Before long a young Hispanic boy joined me. I offered to share with him the bench I was lying on, but he said no, he'd lie on the floor. And for the rest of the night he did lie on the floor, underneath the bench.

My face and head still hurt from being roughed up by the cop. I felt incredibly lonely and afraid. I had no memory of what I'd done the past evening. But somehow amid the noise and the stench, with some criminal I'd never met lying underneath me, I fell asleep for a couple of hours.

At 8:00 A.M. we were awakened by the corrections officers and told to get ready to go to the Bronx Criminal Court Building. We each received a hard roll with butter on it, and a cup of very weak tea. Soon they handcuffed all twelve or thirteen of us together in a line, like a chain gang, and shoved us into the back of a van.

As we sat in the van, the young man who had been strung out on crack noticed me right away. (Because I hadn't washed yet, I still looked bloody and dirty, and I'm sure I looked terrified.) With genuine concern in his voice, he said, "Hey, are you all right?" It was a simple expression of caring, but it meant a lot to me at that point.

In the Bronx Criminal Court Building, they finger-printed me, took my mug shots, frisked me, and went through my wallet. I also had to fill out some forms. On one was the question, "Are you a homosexual?" Afraid that something would happen to me if I told the truth, I checked the No box. Then I was taken to another holding cell.

Maybe they'll lock me up and no one will ever find me, I worried. It was Sunday. I was supposed to show up for work the next morning, and none of my friends knew where I was. My family was a thousand miles away. I begged a security guard to let me use the phone, but he refused.

The court house cell was larger than my first cell, but instead of just one roommate, I had six—all of whom were forced to share one sleeping bench. Each evening there was a scramble, and whoever got there first would claim the bench, and the rest of us had to lie on the floor. Most of my cellmates were young black or Hispanic men who had been arrested on drug charges. From their nonchalant attitude I quickly gathered that most of them had visited this jail many times. They also seemed to get out of jail quickly. I stayed there Sunday, Monday, Tuesday, and Wednesday nights even though the law states that a person must be arraigned within forty-eight hours.

I spent that time sitting in a corner of the cell, frozen in fear that someone would abuse or attack me. Apart from my fear, I felt emotionally numb most of the time. I guess I steeled myself not to feel any of the pain, hurt, and deep anguish that lay beneath the surface. My life was a mess, and now everything had come to a head. I wanted the quickest way out, but I didn't see any way out.

I avoided talking to anyone in my cell, except for one older Hispanic man who, I noticed, was reading his Bible. I said something to him, but quickly realized that he didn't speak English. A few guys asked me what I was in for, and I said, "vehicular assault and drunk driving." Most of them just left me alone.

Twice during my time in that cell the corrections officers came back for another set of fingerprints; they claimed my prints weren't clearing their identification procedures. Because I'd never been arrested before and didn't have any criminal record, they were having trouble positively identifying me. At least that's the excuse they gave for holding me for so long.

After three days in the basement of the criminal court building, I was still waiting to be taken before a judge. I finally convinced a corrections officer to let me out of the cell just long enough to make a phone call—at last! I would have called my close friend Tony first, but I couldn't contact him at work. So I called Tony's brother and left a simple message: "Tell Tony I'm in the Bronx jail and I need a lawyer."

On Thursday I was finally told I would be arraigned by the judge. Since I didn't have a lawyer, they first arranged for me to speak with a legal aid lawyer. Going up the stairs for the meeting, my hopes rose. *Maybe this legal aid lawyer will understand how ridiculous it is for me to be here*, I thought.

To my chagrin, the meeting turned out to be cold, short, and perfunctory. I realized immediately that this legal aid lawyer was simply trying to ram cases through the court as fast as he could.

"How much bail can you afford?" he asked me.

"I don't know," I said, "Maybe one thousand dollars."

He shook his head. "These are pretty serious charges—I don't know if the judge will go for that low a figure."

I was then taken back to my cell, where I waited in a state of near-despair to be called before the judge. When my turn finally came, a corrections officer handcuffed me behind my back and brought me upstairs to a small courtroom. I still wore the same jacket I had on when the police picked me up.

"What are the facts of this case?" the judge said in a routine monotone to the district attorney.

The DA recited all the charges.

"What is your recommendation?" the judge asked.

The DA said, "We think that bail should be set at somewhere between ten thousand and twenty thousand dollars." I gasped.

Then the judge turned to my legal aid lawyer. "Well, what do you want to do?"

"This is a first offense, Your Honor," my lawyer said. "The man says he can come up with one thousand, and I understand that is probably too low. I would recommend five thousand."

"Bail is hereby set at five thousand dollars," the judge said with a tap of his gavel.

Immediately I was escorted out of the courtroom. Though relieved that bail was not as high as the DA wanted, I still wondered where I'd ever come up with five thousand in cash—that day. Unless I was able to put up the money immediately, I knew I'd go back to jail until I could pay. And jail meant Riker's Island, one of the foulest and most-feared penitentiaries in the country.

In the hall outside the courtroom, the legal aid lawyer said to me, "Do you have any way of getting a certified check here immediately?"

"No way!" I said in frustration. "I don't have five thousand in the bank. I have less than one thousand in my account."

He shrugged. "Well, I guess that means you're going to Riker's Island."

I didn't know what to say. I stood there in silence for a moment, looking up and down the hall, wondering what to do. At one end of the hall I saw the corrections people already lining up guys who had gone before the judge but couldn't post bail, getting ready to take them to Riker's Island. *Riker's Island* . . . the very name filled me with terror.

Then I panicked. "Please help me," I pleaded with the lawyer. "I'm scared to death of going to Riker's Island. Can't you do something? I'm not a criminal—I've never been in jail before. I'm afraid I'm going to get caught up in the bureaucracy of the system and never get out."

The legal aid lawyer looked at me and said, "Well, let me go talk to the judge." I waited in a little room right off the courtroom.

A few minutes later he returned. "The judge agrees

with me that five thousand dollars is too high,'' he said. ''So he's reduced it to twenty-five hundred dollars.''

Again, I didn't know what to feel. The legal aid lawyer had helped me, but the twenty-five hundred dollars bail might as well have been twenty-five thousand. I still had to go to Riker's Island. There was no way I could avoid it now.

From the Bronx Criminal Court Building we were then taken to the Bronx Detention Center and processed for entry into Riker's Island. We walked into a large, open room with a large desk in the middle, and holding cells around the perimeter. After people were processed, they would go into a cell.

There were more forms to fill out and questions to answer. When a nurse took a blood sample and a doctor examined my ears and throat, I was petrified that they would find out about AIDS. As far as I know, they didn't. (Or maybe they did and never told me.)

Next I had to submit to the humiliating ordeal of a strip-search. Two by two, they took us into a room, told us to remove all our clothes and put them on a table. One guard rummaged through all the clothes. The other guard told us to bend over, spread our ''cheeks,'' and squat. Apparently some prisoners try to smuggle drugs or razor blades into jail by putting them in a small container and shoving it up their rectum. Squatting forces it out. I don't think I've ever had a more humiliating experience in my entire life.

I put my clothes on and was taken back to my holding cell. While sitting there, I thought more about what would happen on Riker's Island. The prison has a reputation of being a real hellhole. Inmates are sometimes shot and killed there. Only a few months before, I had read in the paper that someone had poisoned the food there, killing several people.

A brief commotion outside the nurse's station

interrupted my thoughts. Someone was escorting a shirtless prisoner from the upstairs jail cells. He was covered with razor slash marks, and blood ran down his chest. He must have gotten into a fight and was now waiting to see the nurse. That scene did little to ease my fears—and we hadn't even gotten to Riker's Island yet.

As I watched everyone being processed, I noticed that prisoners were assigned to different groups. My group—all of whom stayed in one cell—seemed to be mostly young guys in on drug charges. (I was forty-six.) Still afraid that something might happen to me, I began to wonder how I might be assigned to a safer group (if there was one)—or better yet, have my own cell. Then that form came to mind, the one I had filled out earlier where I indicated I wasn't homosexual. *Maybe it is in my best interest to tell them that I am gay*, I thought. *Then maybe they would isolate me and I'd be safer.*

So I looked for one of the uniformed guards to talk to. They were easy to spot, since they looked just like police officers: navy blue pants, light blue shirts . . . and a gun.

I caught the attention of one of these guards, and he came up to my cell. "I filled out one of the forms wrong," I said through the bars. I tried to keep my voice low so the other guys in my cell wouldn't hear, but because of the other activity in the room the guard didn't quite hear me, either. I was nervous because I didn't really know what might happen if either the corrections officials or the guys in my cell found out I was gay.

Finally the guard understood enough of what I was trying to say that he let me come out of the cell and took me over to a private place with one other guard. "Now, just what are you trying to tell me?" he said.

"You know the question on the form that asks whether you're homosexual?" I said. "Well, I answered no, but actually I am homosexual. Should I have said yes?"

Though I saw my share of macho, brutal guards during that experience in jail, I did meet a few compassionate ones. This guy happened to be one of them. "At Riker's you'll be in a cell block with mostly young, first offenders," he said. "You're probably safer there. You don't know what homosexuals in prison are like. You're probably in better hands by not going into the gay cell."

Feeling a little better, I thanked him.

"No problem," he said assuringly. "Look, in the future when you want to divulge some information like that, just say to the officer, 'Can I talk to you in private?' Then it won't look like you're trying to hide information from the other people in your cell. For now, go back to your cell and just act normal. You shouldn't have any problem with the other prisoners."

Encouraged by the guard's caring advice, I went back to my cell. But my feeling of comfort didn't last long. I still knew that in a matter of hours I'd be headed for Riker's Island. It didn't matter whether the guys in my cell block were younger than I—I could still be attacked, beat up, maybe even raped. I could die from food poisoning. That night, with the other prisoners sprawled around me, I lay awake on the cell floor, paralyzed by fear.

Sometime in the middle of the night the guards came around and said, "Okay, get up—we're going over to Riker's Island." The dreaded time had come. They handcuffed us and marched us down a back stairway to the garage, where an old, blue bus stood. Dark blue letters on the side spelled out NEW YORK CITY DEPARTMENT OF CORRECTIONS.

The bus was built like an army truck. All of the windows had heavy mesh screens on the inside of the glass. We were handcuffed and seated two by two in these dilapidated seats, many of which had no cushions. I sat on a bunch of springs along with a young Hispanic kid I was cuffed to, and prepared for a very bumpy ride.

Between the bus driver and the seats was a heavy glass door that, I imagine, protected him from violent prisoners. Once they got us all on board, the driver slammed that door shut with a bone-chilling *clang* that rocked the whole bus. I'll never forget that sound. Then a guard unlocked the garage door, and our bus pulled out of the Bronx Detention Center into the night.

Riker's Island lies at the mouth of the East River, south of the Bronx, and is accessible only by a bridge (closed to the public) that connects the island to the north side of Queens. As the bus bounced and jolted us around in our seats, I recognized some of the city lights and highways along the way. But as we approached the bridge to the island, I saw fewer and fewer lights, and on the bridge it was nearly black. Other than for a brief conversation with my handcuff-partner, I had looked out the window in silence, trying to imagine what it would be like on Riker's Island.

The prison compound is a big place with many buildings of various sizes. We made numerous stops to deliver some guys to whatever cell units they had been assigned. My partner and I were among the last group to be let out.

We were taken to a small processing center with an open room and a TV set. Our cuffs were removed. Initially, the place didn't seem quite as frightening as I had anticipated. Most of the night we sat in the TV room waiting to be processed and assigned to a cell block.

On the whole, I found the corrections officers I dealt with to be pretty compassionate. One officer, in the course of processing me, asked for the details of why I was there and what had happened. "This is your first time?" he said, sensing my fear. When I said yes, he gave me an encouraging look and said, "Aah, you'll be out of here soon."

Once again I had to endure a strip-search, and in the

process I learned what happened to people who didn't cooperate with the guards. One prisoner with an extremely foul mouth kept smarting off to the correction officers. The officer finally said, "Okay, I've had enough of that," and two guards took the man into the room where the searches are conducted. For several minutes I heard the prisoner screaming. When he staggered out of the room, his legs were bloodied; he had been beaten. Though I had been treated well so far, I worried for my safety should some guard happen to be in a bad mood.

We ate a meal of some sort (I couldn't recognize the food) that night while we were being processed. Finally we went to our cell block, which was a large, open, dormitory-style room full of bunk beds, perhaps three hundred beds in all. Despite having my own bed to sleep on, the living quarters terrified me more than did any of my previous cells, because in the cells I never had more than six or seven people to deal with at a time. Now I had three hundred. Anyone could pick a fight with me, or I could get caught in the middle of someone else's fight. People could gang up on me and I'd have no defense. My imagination went wild with fear. I climbed onto the two-inch-thick mattress of my bunk and tried to rest for whatever was left of Thursday night.

Friday morning, the sixth day since my arrest, we ate the standard prison breakfast: a hard roll with a tiny bit of butter, and a paper cup of weak tea. I did nothing but lie in my bunk all day long, getting up only when the guards came to march us to the cafeteria for lunch and dinner. The food was terrible, so I ate very little and I slept a lot.

All those lonely hours in jail during the week, and now at Riker's Island, gave me lots of time to think. *I'm in big legal trouble for running over a girl, and yet I don't remember anything because I drank too much and blacked out. I've missed a week of work without being able to call in and explain. I'll probably lose my job. And I've got*

AIDS—and I'm probably going to die. How am I going to get myself out of this colossal mess?

I had pretty much decided the night after my arrest that I had only one option: to take my own life. Throughout the week I had tried to comfort myself with that thought: *Once I get out of here, I'll end it all.* There at Riker's Island, lying in my bunk, I spent my time planning how I would do it. I figured the easiest way—and a way that I could bring myself to do—would be to slash my wrists, just like in the movies. These ideas gave me an odd sense of comfort and resignation. I didn't have second thoughts. Once Tony came through with the bail money, I knew what I would do.

Like the Prodigal Son, I chose to take my share of my father's inheritance and go into a far country. Even though I was born into a rich spiritual inheritance, even though I was blessed with a beautiful, loving wife and a precious daughter, even though God had opened doors for me and was preparing me for a lifetime of Christian service—even though I had all of this, I chose to take my inheritance, leave my father's house, and go into a far country.

From a sermon Tom preached in 1988

TWO
TWO
TWO
TWO
TWO

It was the first time I'd ever been in jail, but not the first time I had felt hopelessly trapped.

On Sunday nights in seventh grade, I'd lie wide awake on my bed—much the same as I now lay in my jail bunk—dreading having to face the next day. Monday meant going back to school, and going to school meant being around other boys. They stirred up such strange, shameful feelings in me—sexual arousal on one hand and fear on the other. I felt so much safer and more comfortable around girls.

These feelings had begun long before seventh grade. For most of my growing-up years, I had felt trapped by homosexual urges I never asked for and didn't want. In many ways, my early childhood paralleled what some have described as the "classic" upbringing for many homosexuals.

As a kid, you don't analyze what's going on; you can only feel and experience and take everything in. Looking back, I recall various images, feelings, encounters. At the time, I didn't see how they all fit together or how they affected me, but as I describe them now they add up to a pretty clear picture of the origins of my homosexual orientation.

I remember almost nothing about my father before I was four or five, except for brief glimpses of him preaching in a little country church. What I do remember is *wanting* him—wanting him to hold me, spend time with me, talk to me, tell me that he loved me. But he never seemed to have time. He seemed to be too busy or too tired or simply not home.

An old 8mm home movie painfully captured this dynamic between my father and me. We were walking out the front door of the house to go to church. Dad and Mom wore their Sunday best clothes, and I hopped on the porch steps around them, gawking at the camera. I tried to hold my father's hand, but he kept brushing me aside. I got the distinct feeling that my father was ashamed of me.

Why was Dad so unavailable? About the time I was born in 1940 he had experienced a spiritual awakening. He decided to give up his successful pie-baking business in the Midwest to pursue the ministry. Since he had never finished high school, however, he needed to spend four of my early childhood years in a full-time, accelerated study program to earn his high school and college degrees. For two of those years, he lived away in a college dorm, coming home only on weekends to serve as interim pastor for a small nearby church.

In contrast, I remember being surrounded by my mother's affection and protection. She was always around, always there for me. When something made me cry, I always ran directly to her. She'd hold me and stroke my hair, telling me not to worry, that everything would be all right. Mom seemed to be the only one I felt safe around.

I remember feeling effeminate at a very early age. I enjoyed playing with dolls, and liked to dress up in my mother's clothes and parade around the house. Jerry and Peggy laughed at me and called me a sissy. I had a sense that I was different, but didn't know why.

Fear and insecurity accompanied my effeminate tendencies. I didn't like to venture out and make friends, especially with boys. I didn't know how to act around kids my own age. (Peggy and Jerry were six and eight years older than I, respectively, and had their own friends.)

First grade introduced all kinds of trauma into my life. Many mornings I cried and begged my mother to let me stay home. At school, recess terrified me because I had to mix with all these other kids my age. I'd cry and carry on until the playground monitor would take me to Peggy. Other times I'd make such a fuss that my teacher would have to walk me to Peggy's classroom and pull her out of class to come and calm me down.

I settled down somewhat during the next few years. Still afraid of boys, however, I adjusted by spending all my time with the girls, with whom I felt much more comfortable. At recess, I'd play all the girls' games—foursquare, jumprope, dodgeball—instead of joining the boys on the baseball field.

My fourth grade teacher, the first male teacher I'd had, noticed that I always played with the girls, and decided one day to make a spectacle of me. We had just returned from recess, and before the entire class he poked fun at me, saying that I ought to get out more with the boys on the ball diamond.

Everyone laughed. I put my head down on my desk, pretending to laugh, too, but actually I cried. After school I went home and told my mother what had happened. She was outraged, and called my father into the room. "This kind of thing should not be happening," she told Dad. "You're going to have to go talk to Tom's teacher."

In my family no one ever talked about awkward or difficult issues—they were usually either denied or ignored. My mother, I could tell, was sensitive to my effeminacy problem, but mostly tried to protect me from others who made fun of me. I felt that neither of my parents made an effort to deal with my underlying needs.

In this case, Dad shrugged at Mom's statement and then called Jerry, who went to the high school next door to my elementary school. "Jerry," he said, passing the buck, "Why don't you stop by Tom's classroom before school tomorrow. Tell his teacher that Tom's very sensitive, and ask him to be more careful about what he says."

As far as I knew, that was the extent of Dad's involvement. The next day I got to school early and ran to the end of the schoolyard between the elementary and high school to wait for Jerry. The first bell rang. No Jerry. Then the late bell. He was nowhere in sight. I never found out whether he actually spoke to my teacher. The subject was never mentioned again by Jerry or my parents.

I did end up forcing myself to play ball with the boys, however, though not very well. I'd hear chuckles if I tried to throw a ball overhand, but I found that I could pitch underhand without much difficulty. So the boys usually designated me as the pitcher, which I didn't mind at all. At least my ego and self-esteem improved a little.

For the most part, the other kids in school didn't tease me too much. I knew they thought I was different, because every now and then someone would make fun of me. I'd run to my mother, and she'd hold me and say, "You just ignore people who say things like that."

At home Jerry teased me mercilessly. Eventually he just ignored me altogether. Whenever I tried to talk to him or ask a question, he'd say, "What are you doing, kid, writing a book or something?" Then he'd walk away. Sometimes Peggy razzed me, too, but I still felt that she cared about me and loved me as a big sister. We weren't particularly close, but at least I felt that she watched out for me. Actually, I felt closest to my little sister Paula who was six years younger than I. She idolized me as her big brother, and I gave her lots of attention.

In my relationship to my dad, however, I continued to feel a great void. All this time he had been working very hard to provide for the family. His small pastorate paid so little that he had to start another pastry business to make ends meet. And on top of this he was still completing his seminary coursework by correspondence. Eventually, after he sold the business, obtained a full-time pastorate, and finished seminary studies, I saw more of him around the house. But I still felt he didn't pay much attention to me.

School had finally become easier for me to handle, and I began to get involved—especially with performance-oriented activities. I played clarinet in the orchestra, and participated in some of the school plays. I'd look out from the stage and find my mom in the audience, but I never remember seeing my dad.

At age ten or eleven, I didn't give much thought to spiritual matters, even though I was a preacher's kid and went to church twice every Sunday. Everyone's dad had a job, I figured, and my dad's was being a minister. One Sunday night, however, I had an experience that affected me very deeply.

I don't remember what Dad was preaching on, but at some point during the service I felt several strong convictions. One was about boys: I had begun to feel attracted to some of them at school. I didn't understand what this feeling was—I had never heard the word *homosexual* before—but I knew it meant something that wasn't normal. I figured it must be bad, and that I must be bad, and that I needed to ask God to forgive me.

My other conviction was that I wanted to give my life to Christ and become a minister. I didn't know exactly where that conviction came from. Part of it, I'm sure, was real. The other part, I think, came from that empty place in me that I so desperately wanted my father to fill. If I could have expressed what I was feeling in that part of myself, I probably would have said, *Maybe if I accept Christ and become a minister, I'll be more like my father and he'll pay more attention to me.*

At the invitation, I walked to the front and knelt

before my father at the altar. He had a big smile on his face. But he never asked me about it afterward. Neither did anyone else in my family.

Seventh grade stands out as one of the most traumatic years of my childhood. My attraction to other boys had grown stronger, and it caused incredible pain and anguish in me. I wanted to avoid school altogether because it meant being around boys. I had the distinct feeling that something was wrong with me.

For instance, the school desks in my class were arranged in rows, one behind the other. As I sat at my desk, my knees would sometimes touch the back of the boy sitting in front of me. This brief contact would sexually arouse me. I didn't like it; I was afraid. I knew something was wrong, but I didn't know what to do.

One day Jerry came home and told everyone that some older guy had made a pass at him. He couldn't believe that a guy would do such a thing. The rest of the family didn't say much; they basically dismissed the subject. At one point, however, Jerry used the word *queer*. I wondered what that meant.

After dinner I asked my mother. She said it wasn't a very nice word, but it was a boy who was attracted to other boys. *So that must be what's wrong with me*, I thought, *I'm a queer*.

This new revelation only fueled my inner trauma. I forced myself to endure each week of school, and longed for the weekends. Sunday nights the sheer dread of having to return to school the next morning made it difficult to sleep. One Sunday my mother must have heard me tossing in bed, and she came into my room.

"Tom, are you all right?"

I considered telling her that I was fine, but my turmoil was so great that I had to say something.

"Mom, I think something is wrong with me."

"What do you think it is?"

"I don't know. I—I feel attracted to other boys." It sounded like such an awful thing to say.

Then my mother said, "Just a minute. Let me wake your father."

Sitting around the kitchen table that night, I tearfully explained that for some time now I had been feeling sexually attracted to boys, and that I felt terrible about it. I told them I didn't know what to do, and that I hated going to school because of the boys.

They each responded differently to my confession, but the effect was the same. Dad passed it off. "Oh, that's nothing," he said. "I can remember feeling that way when I was your age, too." I think he viewed it as merely a stage, or perhaps part of going through puberty. He was trying to help me feel better.

Mom, on the other hand, had a much stronger reaction. "No you *didn't* feel that way," she said sternly to Dad. "I *know* you didn't." She wouldn't even allow the possibility that Dad could have had those feelings—which, of course, meant that I couldn't have them, either. The message came through clearly.

In a way, it was an odd reaction for Mom, since she had appeared to be more understanding of my effeminacy and my playground struggles of earlier years. Probably she had harbored her own fears that I might be homosexual, but had trouble accepting the truth when I admitted it. Nevertheless, I didn't feel understood by either of my parents. Dad brushed the whole thing aside, and Mom essentially told me I wasn't allowed to feel what I was feeling. Both responses amounted to denial.

Our conversation lasted about forty-five minutes. At the end, they told me not to worry. "Just pray about it," they said, "and it will go away."

That very night and every night afterward for a long time, I knelt next to my bed and asked God to take these feelings away. I was afraid of what they meant. I didn't want to be labeled a queer. So I did everything I could to suppress my desires whenever they arose. The instant a sexual thought popped into my head, I'd steel myself and put it out of my mind. I figured that by praying every night and using sheer willpower, I could overcome my problem.

It didn't work. Sometimes I successfully buried my feelings, but other times my frustration and desperation grew nearly unbearable.

One Saturday afternoon when I was in eighth grade, I went to a movie by myself. As I walked into the theater, an older man followed me in and sat in the row behind me. I didn't look directly at him, but I sensed he was somehow interested in me. After the movie started, I felt something between my legs. This man was trying to massage my crotch, under the seat with his foot.

I froze in fear.

He did it several times. After each time he'd get up and stand in the back of the theater. Then he'd return and do it again. I was getting the message that he wanted me to follow him. I didn't want to—and yet I did.

Herein lay a tragic by-product of my early childhood upbringing: A man was inviting me to be molested, and I was considering saying yes. I wish I'd known what was going on in my psyche at that time: that my basic need for my father's affection had never been met; that I had been subconsciously looking to other boys and men to meet it; and that my male sexual attraction was an extreme expression of my yearning for fatherly attention. That need was even driving me to consider this bizarre sexual encounter.

In spite of my fear the tug of desperation in me prevailed. I mustered the nerve to get up and follow the man into the men's room. For a minute he didn't do anything. Then I realized by the way his eyes shifted that he was nervous, and maybe didn't want to go through with it. I stood there trembling in silence, yet I was sexually aroused at the same time. I wanted to say to him—*Don't leave me now. Please don't leave me.*

A moment later he disappeared without touching me. My heart pounded, and I felt relieved, excited, afraid, and abandoned all at the same time. If he had tried to molest me, I'm sure I would have let him.

That was the closest I came to an overt homosexual experience for the next four years. In high school I felt turned on to other guys frequently, but learned how to conceal my desires. I had overcome my fear of boys, and now enjoyed being around them. I came up with ways to be physically close to them without their getting the wrong idea. For example, I joined the debate team and found opportunities to give back rubs to the other guys. I also loved sleeping with them when we traveled, even though there was no sexual activity.

Though my fear of boys had diminished, I continued to enjoy being with girls in high school. I still felt more comfortable around them, and usually had a girlfriend. My effeminacy had toned down somewhat, but I never felt sexually attracted to girls. My girlfriends were usually friendly companions and little more. They also served to prevent others from thinking that I might be homosexual— one of the many deceptions I learned.

College proved to be an affirming experience for my self-esteem and my relationships. I made lots of friends, and joined the debate team, the drama society, and the a capella choir. I felt very accepted on campus, and respected by my peers. I somehow outgrew my effeminate mannerisms, perhaps as an attempt to mask my sexual preference. I don't think there was anything about me that someone could have pointed to and said, "See? This guy's a homosexual." I also filled out physically (I had been thin and gangling through high school).

By now I had begun to accept my sexual preference as something I couldn't change. But for the most part, the fear of being found out kept my sexual behavior under control throughout college. Even though I knew there were gay men on campus, I never did anything to intimate that I was one of them. I worked so hard at this, in fact, that I didn't even notice on several occasions when guys came on to me. One guy in the dorm room across from me sat out regularly in his underwear, inviting me to wrestle with him. I did, sometimes, but never went any further. I later realized that he was gay. I also felt attracted to some of the guys in my fraternity, but fear kept me from acting on it. This was a small-town, church-related college where everybody knew everyone else's business. I couldn't risk being found out.

I have said that my behavior was under control *for the most part*. I did have my first sexual encounter during my freshman year. But it took place off campus, even out of town. I stopped by a public library I had visited once during high school. I noticed a few men out front, and had a feeling that something was going on. I went about my business, but as I left the library a man who had been sitting on the steps called me over. He looked to be in his early thirties. He said he was from California, and happened to be in the area because his grandparents had died and he was taking care of their estate.

Then he asked me if I'd be interested in going for a ride with him.

I knew what he wanted. And actually, I wanted it, too—assuming *it* meant closeness, affection, pleasure from a man. My adrenaline flowing, I told him I would.

He took me to a house that I assumed was his grandparents'. Nothing was said other than a little small talk. My heart raced as I nervously undressed and got into bed with him.

The very instant he touched me, I had an orgasm. I could tell I had disappointed him. I felt very ashamed, embarrassed, and afraid. All I wanted to do then was put my clothes back on and get out of there. Without saying a word the man dropped me back off at the library, where I had parked my car.

I must have told him my name and where I went to school, because later in my freshman year he called me at my dorm and asked to meet me. Again I said yes, and he picked me up and took me to a motel room. When I got into bed, the same thing happened as before. I did sleep at the motel that night, however, and had breakfast with the man before he dropped me back off at the campus. I never heard from him again, and participated in no further homosexual activity for the rest of college.

It's hard enough to handle all the new ideas and big decisions one must face as a "normal" student, but it seemed all the more difficult for me with my inner struggles. In the last two years of college, I arrived at two contradictory pairs of decisions that seemed fine at the time, but ultimately sent my life into a twenty-five-year tailspin.

Pair Number One: I decided to shelve my faith, yet I also decided to become a minister.

On the surface, I had maintained the external trappings of my Christian commitment: I belonged to the Christian fraternity (derisively known as the "God Jocks"), even serving as president during my senior year; I sang in the church choir; I participated in weekly chapel services and the mandatory religion class. But actually I had begun to seriously question my religious beliefs.

I realized that not everyone in the world came from a conservative religious family as I did. Most of my student friends weren't religious and couldn't care less about matters of faith. I wondered whether my parents had duped me with all their spiritual platitudes; I came to feel that these were childish beliefs I had outgrown.

This realization was furthered when I found myself accepted, to my surprise, into another fraternity—a social fraternity. At my first "real" fraternity party I took my first drink of alcohol. All of a sudden my new fraternity brothers were clapping me on the back and urging me to have more beers. I heard them say to each other, "Hey, look guys, the God Jock is really one of us! The wimp is really a regular guy!" I got very drunk that night, but loved every minute of it. I had discovered I no longer needed my Christian façade and the approval of my parents. I could have fun instead, and enjoy the acceptance and approval of my peers.

Consciously I hadn't made any connection between my religious beliefs and my homosexual desire, but under the surface I'm sure I was concluding something like this: *I was taught that the Bible says homosexuality is wrong, and that if I pray, my homosexual desires will go away. But I didn't ask for these desires, and when I prayed, they didn't go away. So maybe it's Christianity that's wrong, not my desires.*

So why did I want to become a minister? Not because of my personal convictions, that's for sure. To be honest, I didn't really know what I wanted to pursue as a career. To me the ministry was a "safe" profession. I had lived in a minister's family all my life, and basically knew what it was like. I had excelled in debate and drama, so I knew I could handle myself as a public speaker. It was no more than a profession, a job, to me. My father was pleased, too, at my choice.

Pair Number Two: I decided to actively explore the homosexual lifestyle, yet I also decided to get married.

With the exception of those two off-campus sexual encounters freshman year, I had "behaved myself" as far as pursuing homosexual activity throughout college. My desires hadn't gone away—if anything, they had grown stronger. I felt that I had to find out what the homosexual world was all about.

One day I met my father and one of his minister

friends for coffee. We talked about where I might go for my graduate studies. I didn't want a standard, parish ministry program. I was interested in drama, and wanted a program with a twist.

Dad's friend said, "Why don't you consider attending Union Theological Seminary? They have a strong department in Religion in Drama. It's in New York."

New York, I thought. The idea of going to New York greatly appealed to me. I knew that San Francisco and New York had the largest homosexual populations in the country. If I went to Union, I could learn about the homosexual world and still go to seminary at the same time.

So why did I want to get married? I wasn't completely sure. I had met a spectacular woman by the name of Marsha, and had immediately felt a strong attraction to her. Not a sexual attraction, but an attraction to her personality. She was vibrant and popular; she flashed a wonderful smile when she laughed, which was often. From the very start I had pursued her because something about her had really excited me. She had happened to be attracted to me, too.

During our courtship, I had enjoyed "making out," but had never permitted it to go beyond kissing and hugging. I had no interest in touching her in more intimate ways, and didn't want her to touch me, either. But I did feel that I loved her.

When we were both juniors, I had asked her to marry me, and she had said yes. I hadn't breathed a word to her about my homosexual tendencies. I think I had unconsciously hoped that if I married her, they would go away. We had set the wedding date for the August after our graduation, a year and a half away. I had applied to Union Theological Seminary, and in my senior year had been accepted.

Now, as the wedding date drew closer, I was having

serious reservations about marriage. I had already planned to explore the gay lifestyle, and didn't intend to change my mind. But I also felt that I loved Marsha. If I married her, I would have to live a double life. Many times I wanted to call off the wedding, but I couldn't bring myself to do it. So I did nothing—except worry.

August 25, 1962, finally arrived, and Marsha and I married. I had difficulty performing sexually on our honeymoon, but Marsha chalked it up to the newlywed jitters. We moved to New York and settled into a tiny student apartment at Union with one community kitchen and community bathrooms on each floor. I enrolled in my classes. And I set out to find the gay bars.

My double life was about to begin.

Misfortunes are the refining fires from which our spirits and characters are molded, the challenging crises which are calling us to a deeper level of maturity and self-understanding. They are the lessons by which we are taught not only to deal with life's frivolities, but life's tragedies as well.

It is a proven fact that a crisis in a marriage relationship may be the open door to a new and deeper spiritual union between two partners, rather than a destructive force tearing them apart. It is a proven fact that a serious accident in the life of a teenager may be the cause of a sober and newfound maturity. . . .

In the heat of the moment, when the discordant note of tragedy strikes most clearly, it is difficult if not impossible to see the fortune in our misfortune. In the heat of the moment it is difficult to think anything but that we have been forsaken by God. And in that moment there is perhaps only one thought that can comfort . . . that no matter how great our misfortune, no matter how unloved we may feel, we are never divorced from the love of God [Romans 8:38–39]. No matter how vehemently we may curse God, no matter how vigorously we hold God accountable for our misfortune, he will never take away from us his love.

From "God's Inequity," a sermon Tom preached in 1967

THREE
THREE
THREE
THREE
THREE

Besides eating, sleeping, and planning my suicide, I did one other thing during my time at Riker's Island. I used the phone to get back in touch with my friend Tony, since I hadn't heard back from him before being transferred to this jail. On Friday I told him what had happened and that I didn't have enough money in my checking account to make bail. He said he'd try to pull the money together somehow. *Fat chance*, I thought as I hung up the phone. But I was moved by Tony's willingness to help.

To my surprise, Tony showed up at the prison late Saturday afternoon with a cashier's check for my twenty-five hundred dollars bail. He had talked to a few friends and borrowed the additional money. I completed some paperwork, was reminded that I had to appear in court on January 29 (about two-and-a-half weeks), and was then released nearly six days after being arrested. Tony drove me from Riker's Island to his apartment, where I stayed Saturday night. Sunday morning I went back to my place in Connecticut.

When I picked up the phone to call my boss that day, I realized that because I had taken the week off between Christmas and New Year's, I hadn't spoken to anyone from my office since December 24. I worked for Cooperative Educational Services, an agency that served the public schools in southern Connecticut. Today was January 11. I had missed the entire last week of work, and no one had any idea where I was. I was nervous about talking to my boss—especially calling him at home on a Sunday—because I hadn't known him very long. He had only worked at the agency for a few months before the accident, and we hadn't yet established much of a relationship. Taking a deep breath, I told him what had happened. (I didn't mention that I had AIDS—I couldn't bring myself to tell anyone yet.) Though he wasn't too happy that I had disappeared without calling in and that I was now facing felony charges, he still let me come back to work.

In spite of my boss's cool reception, I managed to go to work for the next few weeks. But I did virtually nothing else. After work I'd go straight home, down a few beers until I fell asleep, and then repeat the same pattern the next day. Another friend of mine, Andrew, who knew about the accident and that I had AIDS, came to stay with me.

During this time I continued to seriously contemplate suicide. I had virtually given up. I knew I'd have trouble actually going through with it—I wasn't sure I had the courage. But I was convinced there was no other hope, no other way out. I had no defense for the accident; there were eyewitnesses. And the most serious charge against me—vehicular assault in the first degree—carried a mandatory jail sentence of four to seven years.

I would say to myself, *Tom, it's over. You have no choice. Unless you want to face the possibility of dying in jail of AIDS, you'd better get yourself out of this misery as quickly as you can.*

I felt like a zombie most of the time, my energy sapped by severe depression. With my remaining ounces of strength I managed to get myself to work each day, while inwardly I tried to muster the courage to kill myself. Andrew's presence provided me with a little bit of company, which I appreciated, but I didn't share with him any of my suicide plans.

At one point I made a halfhearted attempt to find a lawyer. I visited one attorney who handled specialized and personal injury cases, but was turned off by him completely. He was your typical brusque, New York, cigar-smoking lawyer. *I can't put my life in this guy's hands*, I said to myself. *I don't trust him.* Besides, he was asking for a retainer of at least one thousand dollars, which I didn't have. Yet another door closed: Even if I found a lawyer I liked, I couldn't afford to pay him. My tension and fear grew.

I had visited my doctor once in those three weeks for a pentamadine treatment. Using a mask connected to a compressor, I would breathe in a mist containing the drug pentamadine. The compressor forces the mist into the lungs. Designed to prevent a recurrence of pneumocystis carinii pneumonia—which I had suffered from only two months ago—the treatment is supposed to be given every two weeks.

During this particular visit I asked Dr. Grossman to give me a Valium prescription. I had never requested tranquilizers from a doctor before, but my anxiety had grown to a point where I wanted something to numb the emotional pain I was feeling. He gave me the prescription, no questions asked. From then on I would take a few Valiums each morning in order to "help" me get through work each day.

As my court date drew closer and I still didn't have a lawyer, I thought of my brother Jerry, who lives in Arkansas. Maybe he'd be willing to lend me some money for a lawyer. One day after work—about ten days before the court date—I went home, picked up the phone, and called him.

"Jerry, I've had a serious car accident," I said, explaining the details. I also told him I had been drinking.

"Tom, are you an alcoholic?" he asked.

"I don't think so, Jerry," I said. "I can usually take it

or leave it. I can go for a couple of days without drinking. It's only recently that I've been drinking pretty heavily."

"Well, Tom, I think you are an alcoholic," Jerry answered. "I'm going to get in touch with somebody I know in New York who can help you, and I'm going to ask him to give you a call. You need to go to an AA meeting."

"Uh, okay," I said, "You can have the guy give me a call. But my immediate problem, Jerry, is that I've got to find a lawyer and I don't have any money. Is there any way you could help me out?"

Jerry paused. "Tom, I'm going to have to think about it."

The next day Jerry called back. "Tom, I've thought about your request," he said. "I know from my own experience that probably the worst thing I could do is help you financially right now. I'm sorry, but I just can't." At first I was angry at Jerry's answer. But a bigger part of me was relieved. If he had given me the money, then I would have had to find myself a lawyer. And that would have complicated my suicide plans. By saying no, however, Jerry provided the confirmation I needed to go ahead. *Well, I'm glad you said that, Jerry,* I mused, *because now I know what I am supposed to do.*

Soon after that phone call I told my friend Tony what Jerry had said. "That bastard!" Tony sneered. "What kind of a brother is he? Give me his phone number—let *me* talk to him." (Tony is Italian, and can have a hot temper at times.)

"No, I don't think so," I said. But somehow Tony found out Jerry's number. I think he called Andrew at my apartment when I wasn't there and got it.

Without telling me, Tony called my brother and said, "Do you know what you've just done?"

"Yes I do," Jerry said. "Tom got himself into this, and he's got to get himself out. I can't help him."

"But Jerry," Tony pleaded. "It's not what you think. Tom has AIDS."

Shortly after I got home from work, the phone rang. It was Jerry. "Tony called me," he said, with more concern than usual in his voice. "Is it true?"

Right away I knew that Tony had told him. And for some reason I wasn't angry. "Yes, it's true, Jerry. I have AIDS."

"Well, that alters the picture somewhat, Tom," he said. "I'm going to have to reconsider my decision about the money. I still don't know whether I can help, but in the meantime I do want you to go to an AA meeting."

"Oh, and one other thing," he continued. "Do you mind if I call Peggy?"

Peggy, my older sister. The one who's the most different from me of all my siblings, yet the one I've always felt closest to. As a kid, I remember her baby-sitting me a lot. As I grew older, I always sensed her watching out for me. There was a special bond between us.

Like me, Peggy hadn't had an easy life. She married right out of high school, had five kids in rapid succession, and was then divorced. With no college education, she managed to find a job in Cedar Rapids, Iowa, and raise the kids herself, though not without great emotional and financial struggle.

To make matters worse, Peggy's youngest daughter, Cynthia, had gotten pregnant at age fourteen, prompting a crisis that somehow led Peggy's entire family to undergo a Christian conversion experience. At that point in my life— despite a degree from Union Theological Seminary in New York—I disapproved of most evangelical expressions of Christian faith, especially the fundamentalist-charismatic brand my sister had picked up. Yet even in my cynicism I couldn't deny that their lives had changed as a result of their newfound faith. I had my own explanations for their change, however. They were simple-minded people, I reasoned, and that's why this simple kind of faith worked for them. But it would never work for me. I knew too much.

Whenever Peggy or her kids tried to tell me about their faith, I delighted in picking theological arguments with them. I'd pose difficult questions to them from my biblical criticism courses, knowing my sister wouldn't have an answer. All she would say was, "Well, I don't know about that."

Peggy didn't have all the answers, but she did have one thing that struck me: There was a light in her eyes—a simple, pure light that I couldn't hide from. Whenever I looked at her, that light shone, and deep inside I knew that something genuine was going on in her life—something I didn't yet understand.

One by one Peggy's kids grew up and moved out on their own, but I still kept in touch with them. Peggy eventually remarried to a quiet, warm guy by the name of Gary. I usually saw their family once a year at Christmas.

"Yeah, okay, Jerry—you can call Peggy if you want. . . . See you later. . . . Bye." I hung up the phone with mixed feelings. I knew Peggy cared about me, and I desperately needed someone to care. Yet the more people who found out I had AIDS, the more complicated it would get for me to carry out my suicide plan. I didn't mind if Peggy knew, but I hoped she wouldn't call or try to get involved.

Early the next morning, at around 7:00, the phone rang again. I knew from the sniffling I heard on the other end who it was.

"How are you, Peggy?" I said softly.

"Not very well," she said.

We had a difficult, awkward conversation. She talked and cried for most of the call. I didn't say much, nor did I shed any tears. At that point I didn't want to deal with her feelings or my own. Mostly I felt anxious to get off the phone. I half expected her to try to evangelize me or break into a Christ-is-the-answer sermon at some point, but she didn't. Instead, I felt her deep love and compassion for me.

"You know that the folks need to be told," she said at one point.

"I know."

"We'll have to do a lot of praying about how to do that."

Peggy requested two things from me. First, she asked if I could come to Cedar Rapids and spend some time with them. I told her I'd think about it and see how my schedule looked, even though I knew I'd probably end my life before I saw them again.

Second, she asked if I'd consider meeting with a minister she knew in New York, B.J. Weber. I had heard of him before, because he lived in Cedar Rapids at the time Cynthia got pregnant, and had counseled her during that ordeal.

"I know this B.J. can help you, Tom, if you'll just go and see him," Peggy pleaded gently. "I just know he can help you." That's about the only pressure she put on me in that conversation. *Peggy, it's too simple a solution to go see this B.J.,* I thought to myself. *I've heard your pitch before and I know what you're trying to say. Not only is it too simple, but it's too late. Things have gone too far now.*

What I actually told Peggy, however, was that I'd think about meeting B.J. I took down his phone number and kept it beside my phone.

Another week went by, and I still hadn't found a lawyer. I also hadn't quite mustered the nerve to kill myself. I couldn't do it in my own apartment; I figured I'd take my last six hundred dollars out of the bank and fly off somewhere. *Maybe I'll fly to New Orleans,* I thought. *That's a party town. Maybe I'll just party for a week, go drown myself in alcohol, and then do myself in real quick.*

Several times during that week, however, I picked up that scrap of paper with B.J.'s number and looked at it. Another thought occurred to me: *Maybe B.J. knows a lawyer who would take me on for free. Or maybe B.J.'s got some other connections. Maybe he can get me out of this.* Underneath I also knew that I badly needed an arm around my shoulder. The day before I was supposed to appear in court, I finally broke down and called him from work.

"B.J., my name is Tom Stribling. I don't know if you know who I am. . . ."

"I know who you are, brother," he said.

"I wonder if it would be possible to come and see you," I said. "I've got some problems."

"Sure. When can you come? How about this afternoon?"

I slipped out of work early and hopped a commuter train into New York. I didn't know what to expect from this meeting, and I was afraid. It would be embarrassing enough for me to explain this whole mess to a friend— much more so to a Christian minister. And what would this B.J. guy be like?

Peggy hadn't told me anything about him except that he was a minister and that he had counseled her daughter. But what kind of minister? His office was not in a church but on the seventh floor of an office building in the heart of Manhattan's financial district. He apparently ran a ministry of his own called the New York Fellowship. After some searching, I found the address: 56 Beaver Street, right above Delmonico's, a well-known steak house.

Inside, a man I assumed was B.J. stepped out of his office. He looked about my age with a friendly, boyish face and thinning hair. "Tom? Come on in," he said, shaking my hand. I sat down on a sofa. He pulled his chair out from behind the desk and sat fairly close to me. We made small talk for a minute, but I could tell that he was waiting for me to take the ball conversationally. So I took a breath and started.

First, I told him that I had AIDS. I had hardly gotten the words out of my mouth when I began to cry. Through my tears I told him all about the accident I didn't remember, about my time in jail, standing before the judge, and my court appearance scheduled for tomorrow. The whole time I poured out my story to him I couldn't read any expression on his face. He hardly moved, and didn't say a word. For a second I thought: *This guy—is he even listening to me, or is his mind somewhere else?* B.J. sat back in his chair in a relaxed position, yet he looked me right in the eye, so I figured he was listening and following my story. But he showed no emotion.

Finally, at one point he broke in with an odd question: "Brother, where's your heart with Jesus Christ?"

I didn't like his question. It made me feel very uncomfortable. Besides, it wasn't relevant to anything. I needed help. I needed money. I needed a lawyer. I didn't need Jesus. I didn't want to answer B.J. Instead, I wanted to run from that question as quickly as I could. But to be polite, I gave him an answer.

"I don't believe that Christ was divine," I said. "He was a good man, but not divine. I believe in God, but not in a personal God. I don't think he can be involved with my life or that he is able to care about me." I had hardly finished answering him when B.J. interrupted me again.

"You know, Tom, God never intended for you to be a homosexual."

At those words my back went up in anger. I sat forward on the couch as if I were bracing for a fight. "I don't agree with that," I retorted, my voice on edge. "I didn't have any choice in the matter. I was probably born homosexual, and if I was born that way how can you tell me that God never intended for me to be a homosexual?"

"I hear what you're saying, Tom, and I understand

your feelings," B.J. said. "Maybe God doesn't have anything against your sexual orientation, but he's displeased when you act it out."

For the rest of the conversation, I felt very tense and suspicious. Somehow I got back to the subject of needing a lawyer. He gave me the name of a Christian lawyer connected with the New York Fellowship and said, "Here, go and see this guy. He'll probably help you." He gave me a name—Lee Ahlers. I had no intention of calling him.

I also told him I had been drinking a lot. B.J. asked me if I wanted to enroll in a treatment program. I said yes, I would like to. So he stepped out of his office for a minute, then returned with a slip of paper. "This is the name of an alcohol rehabilitation center my wife Sheila used to work for. I think they can help you. Just call and ask for this doctor."

"Thanks," I said, standing up to leave. "Well, I think I'd better go now."

"Okay. Good luck, Tom, I hope things work out." As I moved toward his office door, B.J. came up and gave me a big bear hug. "I really love you brother," he said. That hug struck a chord in me. It was the first moment that I felt B.J. genuinely cared.

But even if he did care, I still didn't have a lawyer and I was supposed to be in court the next day. Even if I called the lawyer B.J. had given me, I didn't have any money to pay him. As a last-ditch effort, I called Jerry back, because I hadn't yet heard a final word from him. "Tom, I'm sorry," he said, "but I've decided I can't do it."

The final confirmation. Now I really had no other choice but to pack my bags for one last fling, and then end it all.

*T*here is a time for all of us when we are confronted with Christ. And when that time comes we will not miss it, for it is the most devastating experience a man can have. It is like an arrow shot straight to the heart. It is as if the carefully laid façade of our outer selves has crumbled away and we are left in the nakedness of our souls. In that moment we are suddenly aware that we are poor, lonely, and forsaken creatures. . . .

No matter how much wealth we may have attained, no matter how much significance, how much publicity, there is still that place in each of us where we are impoverished, scared, insecure, and unimportant. This is where Christ meets us, precisely at that poorest level of ourselves. And in that devastating moment we are aware of the great abyss which separates us from God.

From "A Pearl in a Field," a sermon Tom preached in 1967

FOUR
FOUR
FOUR
FOUR
FOUR

The evening after my unsettling appointment with B.J., I called my friend Andrew, who had been coming out from New York to stay with me. "Andrew, I need to be alone for a few days. Do you mind just staying home for a while? I'll call if I need you. I hope you understand."

"All right," Andrew said. "I'll probably stop by in a day or two." He had a key to my apartment.

I fell asleep that night with a mixture of resolve and fear: resolve that I had to go ahead with my suicide plan, and fear over whether I'd be able to pull it off. I dragged myself into work the next morning, but couldn't concentrate. As I sat in on a meeting, someone turned to me and asked a question; I couldn't answer because I realized that I hadn't heard a thing that had been said. Excusing myself, I left the conference room, picked up my phone, and made a one-way plane reservation to New Orleans. Then I caught a taxi to the bank, withdrew my remaining six hundred dollars, and went home to pack.

Looking around my apartment for the last time, I realized what a mess it was. I had let it go completely to pot during the last few weeks. I hadn't washed a single dish. I had just piled them in the sink, not even bothering to scrape the food off. The garbage can was overflowing. Empty beer cans sat on the coffee table and kitchen counter. I had strewn my clothes everywhere—over the backs of chairs, on my bedroom doorknob, on my bed. *Oh, well*, I sighed, *Someone else can clean it all up after I'm gone for good*. Grabbing a duffel bag for a suitcase, I haphazardly threw in some underwear, some socks, a pair of jeans, maybe a shirt or two, and a sweater.

Instinctively, I also reached up to the bookcase above my bed and took my Bible—the Bible that I hadn't read in twenty years—and tossed it into my duffel bag. I'm not sure exactly why. Perhaps knowing that I was about to step over the edge into eternity had something to do with it. Maybe I was having doubts. Maybe subconsciously I worried that if I committed suicide, God would punish me with eternal damnation.

Before I left my apartment to catch a taxi to the airport bus, I popped four or five Valiums. Then I scribbled out a short note on the back of an envelope:

> Dear Friends,
>
> I can't handle the things I have to deal with any more. I hope you can forgive me.

I left the note on my desk, not knowing exactly why I had written it. A small voice inside may have been saying, *If I'm not supposed to go through with this, maybe someone will find this note in time to stop me*.

I took the cab to the airport limousine, and then rode for forty-five minutes to LaGuardia Airport. In the back of my mind I was thinking, *When I get to New Orleans, I'm going to fulfill every fantasy I've ever had until my money is gone, and then I'll take my own life*. I picked New Orleans because I had visited there several times before and knew it was a party town. I didn't have any qualms about exposing another person to AIDS. It didn't even enter my mind. I wasn't thinking about other people; I was too caught up in my own despair.

I paid for my airline ticket in cash. It cost one hundred-fifty dollars, which left me with four hundred-fifty.

During the flight I kept thinking, *This is the last trip of your life—this is the end of it all. It's all over.* The only feeling I had was numbness—much of it Valium-induced, I'm sure, but I purposely tried to cut myself off from any feeling. I didn't want to face it, whatever it was.

As the plane drew closer to New Orleans, however, I felt a growing sense of fear, even paranoia. I worried that the police authorities would be looking for me. Since I was scheduled to be in court that day and hadn't shown up, there would probably be a warrant out for my arrest.

But lurking behind my paranoia was an even deeper fear about what I was planning to do to myself. In the back of my mind a voice kept telling me, *Tom, maybe there is a heaven and a hell, and maybe you're just trading a temporary suffering for an eternal suffering. Maybe all the things you were taught as a child really are true.* That fear haunted me on and off over the next few days.

I got to New Orleans, and to avoid discovery, checked into the Marriott under a fictitious name. The Marriott was probably a poor choice given my limited funds, but I had stayed there once before for a conference and I knew it was close to Bourbon Street. The weather outside was hot and humid. I realized I didn't need the jacket I had brought along.

After checking in, I went up to my room and dropped my bag on the bed. It was early afternoon. Without bothering to unpack, I left my jacket in the room and went out to Bourbon Street, looking for a bar. I knew most of the gay bars were at the far end of Bourbon Street, so I walked until I found one. Sitting there at the bar with two or three beers under my belt, I struck up a conversation with the bartender.

"Where are you from?" he asked me in his southern accent.

"Connecticut," I said. But as soon as the word came

out my paranoia struck again. *Oh, no, I shouldn't have said that—they'll find me.*

Immediately I got up and left that bar, thinking that if I left right away the bartender wouldn't remember my face when the police come looking for me. I went into another bar, stayed until I was afraid someone might recognize me, and then left. This pattern continued for several hours. I must have walked the entire length of Bourbon Street three or four times in that sweltering heat before I finally went back to the hotel.

In my hotel room, I had a couple of drinks from a bottle of Scotch I had picked up. As darkness settled over the city, I went back out onto Bourbon Street and hit a few more bars. Then back to the hotel again, where I took a few more Valiums and drank more Scotch until I passed out.

Between the alcohol and the Valium, my activities during the next day or two registered as little more than a blur. I know I didn't eat anything; I probably just went from bar to bar and drank. By this time my fear of being discovered had grown to the point that I decided to leave New Orleans. On the third night I went to the Greyhound station and took an overnight bus to Atlanta. The fare was cheap, and with my dwindling funds, I didn't have to worry about a hotel room that night.

The bus trip was long, grueling, and uncomfortable. I took a few Valiums and tried to curl up in my seat and sleep, but I woke each time the bus stopped—in virtually every Louisiana and Mississippi town it went through. I'd get off and buy a package of peanut butter crackers in the Greyhound waiting room. (I still hadn't eaten since I left Connecticut.) Finally, we reached Atlanta sometime the next morning.

Now what? I thought as I stood in the bus station in downtown Atlanta. I had nowhere to go. I had never been to Atlanta. I didn't know a thing about it. I didn't know where the gay area was. I also knew I had to start watching my funds.

By walking around, I found a cheap motel for about thirty-five dollars a night, and again checked in under a false name. It was a tawdry place. The drapes of my ground floor room didn't close completely, and people walking by could look right in. For the most part, all I did in Atlanta was lie on the bed, getting up occasionally to pour myself another drink. Because it didn't cost much and I felt safe from the police, I must have stayed there three or four days.

As for fulfilling my wildest fantasies, I didn't have much luck in Atlanta. Once or twice I set out on foot to find a bar, but couldn't find anything nearby. Downtown Atlanta at night is completely dead. One night I decided I'd walk as far as I needed to go to find a gay bar, and I took off. Eventually, I tracked down a gay bookstore and got the address of a gay bar. I found the street, but had no idea how far the bar was from the downtown area. I must have walked several miles down that street, but never located the bar. By now it was late at night, so I turned around and trudged all the way back to the motel.

Drinking, sleeping, and aimlessly traipsing around Atlanta left me bored, lonely, and depressed. I wondered where else I could go for a final round of excitement. In addition, my paranoia about the police flared up again, fueling my sense of urgency to move on. *Maybe I'll go to Chicago*, I thought. I'd been there before and knew where some of the bars were. So I called United Airlines and got a special seventy-nine dollar fare from Atlanta to Chicago.

In Chicago I once again checked into a seedy motel on the north side—not quite as seedy as in Atlanta but fifteen dollars more per night. I chose it because I knew that a number of gay bars were in that area—not to mention that Chicago in January is bitter cold and windy, so I didn't want to walk far to find places. Sure enough, I hit several nearby bars and a gay peep show, where I spent quite a while dropping quarters into the peep show machines. I kept up this routine for several days, trying to put out of my mind what I was going to do, yet also knowing it was inevitable.

Most of the time I hung out in a grungy joint on Clark Street known as Stop & Drink. It wasn't a gay bar; I'd call it more of a down-and-outers' bar. I drank beer and struck up a few conversations, but mostly sat around. I also bought a bottle of Scotch from that bar and kept it in my room.

I realized my money would run out soon. My time was near, yet I felt no peace about ending my life. Instead, my inner turmoil raged stronger than ever. Though I was trying to drown myself in alcohol, questions about heaven and hell and eternal punishment consumed my thoughts. *Should I or shouldn't I do it? Is it wrong or is it right? Is there a heaven and a hell? Am I going to hell if I do this?* That was my fear. Yet what other choice did I have? I was going to die of AIDS anyway, and I didn't want to die in jail.

While walking around one afternoon, I noticed the sign for Moody Bible Institute and Moody Bookstore, which happened to be in the same area as my motel. Having been a pastor's kid and seminary trained, I had heard about Moody. To me it was an extremely conservative organization of fundamentalists who interpreted the Bible too literally and lived by a long list of do's and don'ts. Still, as I passed the bookstore, I wondered what answers they'd give to my questions. So I went inside.

On the shelf directly in front of me stood a book entitled *The Christian's Response to Suicide*. I picked it up and started to read. After only two or three paragraphs, I quickly closed the book and put it back on the shelf. *I don't really want to know the Christian's response to suicide,* I thought. *I'm so close to doing it now that I don't want anything to confuse me.* So I left the bookstore. By now I had just enough money for one more night at the motel, plus a little extra. I decided that tomorrow would be the day I would take my life.

That afternoon, I got a strong urge to call my sister Peggy. I knew I hadn't been thinking straight for the past week anyway, but for some reason I wanted to talk to her. Maybe I wanted to tell her good-bye. Or maybe I was crying out for help.

I went to a pay phone on the street and dialed Peggy's number. Just as she answered, however, the operator broke in and said, "Sir, you'll have to drop in ninety-five more cents." Immediately my police paranoia gripped me. *Maybe her phone is tapped by the authorities*, I thought. Panicking, I hung up the phone.

After a few more beers at the Stop & Drink, I got up the nerve to try Peggy again several hours later. I put more change in the phone this time. When she answered, I managed to say, "Peggy, I'm trying to kill myself."

"Tom, you can't do that!" she answered immediately. But then the operator interrupted again for more money. Again I hung up the phone and went back to my room.

The next morning, I knew I didn't have enough money to pay for another night, so I said to myself, *Well, now's the time. Now I've gotta do it.* I went out and bought a bottle of Scotch at Stop & Drink. At a corner drugstore I asked for a pack of single-edged razor blades. Then I went back to my motel room.

First I took about ten Valiums and drank several glasses of Scotch; then I sat on the edge of the bed and waited for the numbness to kick in. I began to feel melodramatic, and tried to imagine how they'd find me after I was dead. The final scene from the movie about Lenny Bruce came to mind, where they found him slumped over the toilet with blood all over the place. He had slashed his wrists, too. That's how I envisioned myself ending up.

Once I felt good-and-numb, I took my clothes off, except for my T-shirt and undershorts. I walked into the bathroom, just as I had seen Lenny do it in the movie. It was a small, old 1950s bathroom that had never been fixed up, with ancient fixtures and tacky green tile. The shower curtain was torn, and the tile was chipped and cracked in places.

I turned on the sink faucet, and took one of the razor blades. Choosing two prominent veins on my left wrist, I sliced across them and then in line with them seven or eight times. It didn't hurt. A small amount of blood flowed, but it seemed to coagulate quickly. I dangled my wrist over the sink, thinking that gravity would help the flow, and waited.

Nothing happened. So I moved to another spot on my wrist and tried for another vein. Figuring I wasn't cutting deep enough, I sliced this vein over and over again. The skin was pulled back, exposing tissue and blood vessels, but very little blood seemed to flow. Slashing at a different angle didn't help, either. Then I made a few superficial attempts at slashing my other wrist, but the same thing happened.

I carried out this whole process very matter-of-factly, with little or no feeling. I numbly went through the motions. But after cutting away at myself for nearly an hour, the thought occurred to me, *I'm not going to be able to do this*. The bathroom still looked clean. The small amount of blood I had coaxed from my arms had already gone down the drain. Other than a few drops on the sink, I had some blood on my undershirt and that was pretty much it. It was a far cry from the Lenny Bruce scene I had imagined.

I began to panic. This is my last resort, my way out of all this misery and suffering, I thought. *What am I going to do now? I can't go anywhere else—I'm out of money*. I lay across the bed, racking my brain for other options.

Across the room I noticed a plastic dry-cleaning bag

hanging in the closet that someone had left behind. Another way out. I put the bag over my head and sealed off the air by tying my belt around my neck. Then I breathed in and out. Just when I could tell I wouldn't be able to get another breath, however, I panicked and ripped the bag off. Somehow it seemed even scarier and more painful to kill myself by suffocation than by slashing my wrists. It's that same feeling of terror you get when you're choking, or when you've gotten caught in the undertow at the beach— that moment when you gasp, *Oh, my God, I'm not going to get another breath!*

I lay on the bed until I had the nerve to try again. Twice more I repeated this routine, each time yanking the bag off at the last second. After three attempts I had shredded the bag to the point of uselessness. I realized I didn't have the courage to die that way.

By then I was beginning to pass out from all the Valium and Scotch. I thought, *Maybe if I lie with my arm dangling off the bed, I'll bleed to death during the night.* So in utter exhaustion and despair, leaving a towel on the floor underneath my arm, I faded into sleep.

Something happened to me in the middle of that night, the loneliest night of my entire life. I think I died—not physically—but a different kind of death. I think I had a taste of what spiritual death must be like: to leave this world forever and have no hope, no answers, no sense of purpose whatsoever.

When I was falling asleep, I really didn't want to wake up in the morning. But I did awaken, and when I did, something was different. My first thought was, *Oh, no, I'm still alive. What do I do now?* I looked at my wrists. The blood had dried and caked around the cuts. There was some blood on the sheets and on the towel I had left. But I was very much alive. Still lying in bed, I toyed with the idea of getting dressed, standing on a street corner until a bus came by, then jumping in front of the bus. *With the luck I've had so far, it probably wouldn't work and I'd end up maimed for life*, I thought.

As I entertained new ways to kill myself, a new awareness rose from within me, an awareness that had come during the night. I realized I didn't want to die. I wanted to live. But how? How could I extricate myself from the mire I had gotten myself in?

At that moment I thought of my sister Peggy again. She didn't have all the answers, and she certainly couldn't solve my legal tangles. But she did stand out in my mind as a ray of hope, as someone who represented life. Yesterday I thought I was in control. I thought I could make it on my own. Today I knew I couldn't. I needed to reach out, to ask someone for help. Maybe there was something, or someone, behind that light in Peggy's eyes.

Climbing out of bed, I pulled off all the sheets and the towel and tossed them into a corner. I went out into the cold to a pay phone and dialed her number one more time. She picked up the phone immediately; I could tell she had been sitting by the phone waiting.

"Tom? Tom!" she blurted out. "Listen, Tom, you have a lawyer in New York, and he said to tell you that no one's looking for you." She spoke very fast so I wouldn't cut her off again. But she said the words I needed to hear; I relaxed. The police weren't coming after me. And it was great to hear Peggy's voice.

Then I heard myself say, "Peggy, I want to come there."

She told me to get a ride to the airport, and that a ticket for Cedar Rapids would be waiting for me at the United terminal. I hurried back to my motel room to pack. I had just enough money for a taxi to O'Hare.

We are told that Christ is "the Word made flesh." And so he is. But what a confusing word he is. One would expect the Word of God to be clear and lucid. But Christ spoke in riddles: "The first shall be last and the last first." He spoke in paradoxes: "He who would save his life shall lose it, but he who would lose his life for my sake shall find it." He was a contradiction: "I came not to bring peace but a sword." One would expect some kind of balanced discourse from the Word of God but his words often contradict themselves. One would expect the Word of God to be original, but these words of Christ were uttered by the Old Testament prophets before him. One would expect some attention to questions such as "Who is God?" and "What is man?" But Christ never offers any definitions.

At best, we can only say what we think these words mean and then we cannot do it with any degree of certainty. Listening for the voice of God in the words of Christ is not enough to satisfy our despair and loneliness. We must accept the fact that for all practical extent and purpose, God is silent in our day. . . .

From "Coping With God's Silence," a sermon Tom preached, and believed, in 1967

FIVE
FIVE
FIVE
FIVE
FIVE

What was it like to live a double life?

I should know. After marrying Marsha and moving to New York, I became an expert on the subject. I had decided to give in to my homosexual desires, and within six months of my wedding I was meeting men regularly in gay bars, going to their apartments and having sex—all without Marsha's knowledge.

What was it like to live a double life?

Deceptive and deceitful. During the day, Marsha worked as a secretary. I often had a few hours to kill between classes, so I'd slip over to the gay hangouts in Greenwich Village, looking for sex. Evenings, I'd tell Marsha I was going to the library to study, and then would go straight back to the Village, returning three or four hours later. To avoid discovery, I never met guys anywhere near the seminary, never mentioned that I was a seminary student, and never used my real name. I compiled my own working list of excuses for going out, and alibis for when I returned too late. I covered myself so well that during my entire four years in seminary, I never once had a close call. And to my knowledge, Marsha never suspected a thing.

Obsessive. What began as an early childhood need for fatherly tenderness had turned into an adult preoccupation with male sex. Because the underlying need had never been met, the adult result had become twisted. At that time, of course, I didn't understand why I had these homosexual desires. I figured I'd been born that way. And ever since junior high, when I had learned what a *queer* was, those desires seemed to have built up in me, year after year, without (for the most part) being expressed. Now the urges were so great that they began to control me, and as I gave in to them the sense of release and pleasure so overwhelmed me that I had to have more. I'm not saying I had no ability to choose whether to have sex— rather, that I felt that I only had one choice—to follow my desires and satisfy whatever that need was inside of me.

In a sense, my yearning for more and more gay sex parallels that of many heterosexuals who, upon discovering how good sex can feel, go for it again and again. I keep using the word *sex* here, as opposed to *love* or a *relationship*. At this stage I wasn't consciously looking for love, or even for a relationship. Basically I wanted sex.

An internal battleground. I continually felt at war with myself. Half of me, it seemed, was doing what I was "supposed" to do: stay with my wife, study for the ministry, keep up the appearances of being happy. The other half of me was doing what I "needed" to do: satisfy that powerful desire, somehow fill the great void I felt. These two "halves" of myself directly opposed each other; they couldn't peacefully coexist inside of me. I didn't know how long I'd last in this kind of battle. Something would have to give.

As my seminary years progressed, I became increasingly convinced that I could no longer stay with Marsha. I still loved her, but I knew our relationship had no future as long as I intended to see men on the side, which I did. By now I had learned to "perform" with her, but I didn't particularly enjoy it; often I had to fantasize I was having sex with a man in order to climax.

Of course, Marsha knew nothing about the struggle

going on in me, about how difficult it was for me to make love to her. Nevertheless, I endured it once or twice a month at most, and used every excuse I could think of to evade it the rest of the time.

In my senior year at Union, Marsha kept bringing up the subject of her getting pregnant—the very last thing I wanted. I feigned mild interest, but avoided making love at every turn. I was having enough trouble maintaining my relationship with Marsha alone; a baby would dramatically complicate things. More and more I believed that staying married would tie me down and prevent me from further exploring this lifestyle I was so drawn to.

We spent my last nine months of seminary in Aberdeen, Scotland, where I had an internship with a church. Scotland is a beautiful country with many wonderful people, but it wasn't New York. Homosexuality seemed much more taboo there, and I found it difficult to meet other gay men. Typically, I'd pick up someone on the street in certain areas, or in public men's rooms. We'd drive to the outskirts of town and have sex in my tiny car, then I'd drop him back off in the city. As in New York, I kept everything completely anonymous. Within a few months I had decided that I couldn't live the double life any longer; I didn't really want to go into the ministry, either. I just wanted to get back to New York and pursue the gay life. Once we returned, I would ask Marsha for a divorce.

Shortly after I had arrived at this decision, Marsha arrived home from the doctor. Her period had been late, and she had gone to take a pregnancy test. They told her to call for the test results later that afternoon. I was terrified. We had made love so seldom that I could hardly believe she could be pregnant. But if she was . . . my worst nightmare could be coming true.

We had no phone where we lived, so we walked down the street to the red wooden phone booth to call the doctor.

I stood outside, pleading with God to make the test results negative. Barely a moment later, Marsha burst out of the booth and threw her arms around me.

"Tom, we're pregnant! We're pregnant!"

My heart stopped. I tried to look mildly pleased when she hugged me, but inwardly I was horrified. I could no longer carry out my divorce plans. Severe depression immediately set in. All I could think was, *What am I going to do now? I can't leave her now, not with a child. What am I going to do?*

I would have to wait.

Fast-forward nine months. Marsha and I had returned to the States, staying with her parents in Iowa until the baby came. She woke me one night and said, "Tom—it's time." Her water had broken. Excitedly I jumped up and drove her fifteen miles to the hospital in her father's car.

In 1966, fathers played no role in the delivery of a child other than sitting in what was then called the Fathers' Lounge. Marsha had a difficult labor that dragged on for twelve or thirteen hours. The doctors finally decided to perform a caesarean operation, which took five hours. I had lots of time to think.

So many conflicting emotions tore at me. A big part of me really wanted a child and felt genuinely excited to have created this new life that I could hold and love and care for. I've always loved children, and enjoyed spending time with my little nieces and nephews. Yet simultaneously I felt like a frightened child myself as I sat there waiting to become a father. The prospect of actually becoming a parent scared me. I was so unprepared; my own life seemed so filled with turmoil and confusion. How would I handle this giant responsibility?

In addition to the burden of impending parenthood, the need to somehow resolve the dilemma of my double life still weighed heavily on me. Marsha still knew nothing about my struggle, though our arguments had diminished when she got pregnant. I had accepted a position as campus chaplain for a large midwestern university; I didn't particularly want the job, but it had become available at the time I needed work. What I really wanted was to return to New York, where I could keep exploring the gay lifestyle.

In the town we were to live in I had already secured an apartment for us. I had also located the area known for "cruising." Men would drive up and down the street and pick up other men. They'd disappear into the bushes for a few minutes, then get back into their cars and leave. I had begun to join in this practice, too, before going back up to Iowa to be with Marsha. But the battle between my homosexual desires and my responsibility to my family continued to rage.

The Fathers' Lounge door opened. A nurse called me in. There in the hospital corridor, in a glass incubator on wheels, I met my precious little daughter, Elizabeth. We would call her Libby. She had a very noticeable ring around her face—a deep impression caused when she pressed against Marsha's pelvic area during labor. I expressed concern about it to the doctor, but he said it would go away "in time."

I arranged to have an extra bed wheeled into Marsha's room so I could stay with her. I had trouble sleeping that night because I kept worrying that Libby might be deformed. The next morning, much to my relief, the ring had completely disappeared.

I loved my little girl. I loved to hold her, play with her, feed her. I even enjoyed the mundane duties such as giving baths and changing diapers. But a terrible awareness also ate away at me as we settled into our apartment and my new job: Libby and Marsha stood in the way of my freely going after my desires.

Shortly after beginning my chaplaincy, the local newspaper ran a story about me and included a photo. Little did I know that this article would ultimately lead to the painful end of my double life. I never thought about the possible repercussions until one day when I arrived home from work.

"You got the strangest phone call today," Marsha said. "Some man wanted to know if you drove a red Dodge Dart. I said yes. Then he said, 'Oh, I thought that was Tom. Just tell him Ray called and that I'll call him back.' "

I pretended to know who Ray was, and acted as though I understood his message. But inwardly, to my horror, I suspected that something very sinister was going on. Ray must have seen me cruising, and then figured out who I was when my picture appeared in the paper.

He wanted to blackmail me.

I trembled at the thought of having my cover blown. We lived in a small, conservative, provincial city that had little tolerance for homosexual behavior, especially in 1966. My parents, who lived nearby and who had helped me get this job, would be devastated if word got out. I'd be immediately fired from my chaplaincy. Marsha would be terribly hurt. My life would fall apart. But for now there was nothing I could do but wait and worry.

Ray called back later that same night. His words struck fear in my heart.

"I know what you've been doing," he said. "I sure don't think the church would be too happy if they knew. And your wife wouldn't be very happy if she knew, either."

Terrified, I abruptly hung up on him. I stood next to the phone, shaking. Marsha saw how upset I was.

"What is it, Tom? Tell me, what is it?" she pleaded.

I could keep my secret no longer.

"Marsha, we've got to talk," I said, sitting down on the living room couch. "I've got to tell you something." As she sat down next to me, I took a deep breath and began.

"I have been struggling with homosexuality ever since I was in seventh grade. I have had sex with other men.

Now, this man who called, Ray, has found out about me and is threatening to tell my employer and to tell you."

She stared at me in silence. I couldn't begin to imagine the depth of her shock: here she was, a young wife with a new baby and a new apartment in a strange town, hearing her husband tell her he's homosexual. Her face registered confusion and hurt and disgust and utter disbelief; it took her a while to absorb what I had just told her.

When I tried to further explain my struggle, she recoiled. "Tom, I can't believe you actually had sex with another man. I don't know if I can ever touch you again," she said. The whole idea of homosexuality repulsed her. Rather than lash at me or leave the house, however, she tried (to my amazement) to listen and be supportive.

Neither of us really knew what to do. She suggested getting some legal help with the blackmail problem, but the bigger issue of our relationship and our marriage remained. I broached the subject of separation and divorce; she said she didn't want to split up. Strangely, we didn't argue. We both cried, though, and when the conversation ended we hugged.

I lived in absolute dread that Ray would call again. At night I couldn't sleep, and Marsha would hold me and comfort me. She seemed to understand my anguish, and yet must have also felt bewildered and betrayed by it.

Ray did call. Though it was clear he wanted something from me in exchange for his confidentiality, he never mentioned money. First, he told me—he called it an "offer"—to come to an orgy.

"There will be other men like you there who are married, and no names will be used. It will be safe."

I said no thanks.

A few days later he called again, this time threatening to tell my superiors at the university. I was beside myself with fear. I knew I had to get some kind of legal help, so I made an appointment with the dean of the university's law school. I told him of my predicament. He was a little taken aback, but he referred me to a more liberal lawyer in town.

"I don't think this guy is going to let you alone," the lawyer told me. "If there is any way you can leave town without drawing much attention, I'd advise you to do so. He sounds as though he is determined to blackmail you."

Altogether, Ray called five or six times over several weeks. On a couple of the calls he acted friendly and didn't threaten me. I finally said to him, "What about all these threats you've been giving me?"

His voice immediately became serious. "Do you have anyone listening in on this phone conversation?" he demanded. "Well, you better not." Then he reissued all the same threats as before.

Quickly I concluded that I had little choice but to follow the lawyer's advice. I told Marsha that we would have to move. Then I contacted the Methodist bishop in my region and requested a transfer. He said he had an opening at a church in Brooklyn, New York, and agreed to make the official arrangements. My parents were dumbfounded at this development, especially since they had helped me get the chaplaincy job. All I could tell them was that I realized I had made the wrong move, and that we were going back to New York. Within a few weeks we had settled into a parsonage apartment in Brooklyn. I never heard from Ray again.

We stayed there for the next year and a half, and I tried to function as a parish minister, something I had never wanted to do. Why? Because I had to teach doctrines I didn't believe, didn't feel in my heart. The questions I had asked in college about my faith were only reinforced at Union Seminary. By the time I had received my Master of Divinity degree, I didn't believe in (or even care about) Christ's divinity. Nor did I accept the truth of the Resurrection or the reliability of the Bible.

In spite of feeling like a hypocrite, I managed to stand

before the congregation and give a sermon each week. Some very much reflected the liberal teaching I had received at Union. Others might even have made my dad proud. On Good Friday, 1967, for instance, I spoke on why that day was known as Good Friday:

> The cross is not a tragedy, it is the saving act of God in history. There is no other single event in history that should cause more celebration, more happy faces, than man's salvation. And man's salvation was the cross.
>
> A well-known picture following the First World War shows a young soldier lying frozen by death in the middle of no-man's-land. He had been sent out there in the midst of the battle to connect a communications cable that had snapped in two when hit by shellfire. The young man was killed, but his death was not in vain, for in his stiffened hands were the two ends of broken cable held tightly together. And the title of the picture is simply, "The Message Went Through."
>
> This picture is a perfect analogy for the crucifixion. Christ's nail-pierced hands held the broken tie that separated man from his Maker. Because of the cross, you and I have been reconciled to our God. The ties that have been broken by our selfishness and stubborn pride have been reunited in Christ's dying hands. No man has better served the needs of humanity by living than did Christ by dying.
>
> Now do you see why today is Good Friday? We are not here to mourn a tragedy. A tragedy is the death that is senseless, serves no purpose, is without meaning. The death of John F. Kennedy was a tragedy. The death of thousands of Jews in Nazi gas chambers was a tragedy. The death of Christ was the salvation of mankind. . . .

At the same time I was preaching these sermons, I had resumed my double life of promiscuity amid the large, anonymous gay population of New York. In such a big, cosmopolitan city I didn't worry about being blackmailed again. Since I had gotten over the hump of telling Marsha I was gay, some of my internal turmoil had quieted down. She had been loving and supportive, but sadly, my agenda for leaving her hadn't really changed.

For a while we went to a marriage counselor—at Marsha's request—but I just went through the motions. Because I had fixed my mind on getting out of the marriage, I didn't allow myself to give our relationship a chance. Neither did I attempt to address the important issues stemming from my upbringing. The counselor finally told Marsha that it seemed obvious that I no longer wanted to be married.

By this time I had asked the bishop to release me of my duties at the church, and I enrolled in a special master's degree program at Union. I kept telling Marsha that I needed to move out and get my own apartment. She'd react with anger and bitterness and desperation, yet she still wanted me to stay. We'd get into long fights late at night over what I was going to do. I'd tell her I couldn't stay any longer, that I wasn't making her happy.

My greatest hesitation in leaving, however, was Libby, who had just turned three. I had spent lots of time with her—playing, reading *Winnie the Pooh* stories, taking her sledding on the hill nearby, driving her back and forth to nursery school each day. I adored her, and she seemed to be very attached to me. Though she never witnessed any discussions or fights between Marsha and me, I was sure she had picked up on the tension in our marriage. Maybe she had heard some of our nighttime clashes after we thought she was asleep. My leaving would be very hard on her—and missing her would be hard on me.

But I had to make a choice, and I was choosing to abandon her and Marsha for a completely different lifestyle, one that I thought would make me happier and give me more freedom. Finally I set a moving date, told Marsha, and arranged to stay with a friend-from Union. I would take very little with me—just a few clothes and personal items.

The day I left, Marsha stood at the door with me and

said, "Tom, I don't want you to go. I don't want you to leave."

"I'm sorry, but I have to. I don't have any other choice."

I looked down at Libby, who was standing next to her. I knelt down and said, "Libby, your mother and I have decided it would be better if Daddy had his own apartment for a while. So I am going to be moving. I'll still come and see you, and we'll still spend time together."

I'll never forget the look on her face—the terror and hurt in her eyes. We had done nothing to prepare her for this traumatic moment. And now, with no warning, her daddy was walking out on her. As I turned and left, I knew that expression on her face would haunt me for years to come.

*   *   *

Finally, at age twenty-eight, I was on my own. Free from my family responsibilities, free from the confines of the church, free from having to preach a gospel I didn't believe. And most of all, free to pursue the life that had been calling me for so long—the life of unbridled homosexual pleasure and fulfillment. No longer would I allow someone else to control me or limit me. No longer would I have to live a double life, except perhaps in my job. Now I was in charge of my life. Now I could be truly happy.

I dived into the gay lifestyle headfirst.

Eighty percent of my free time I spent chasing after sex and drugs and the social scene. On a typical Saturday evening I'd find a few friends and hang out at the gay discos, where we'd get sky high on mescaline (and, in later years, cocaine) and dance the night away. When we didn't go to the bars and discos, we'd check into the gay bathhouses, which embody every image one can envision of sexual debauchery. In these places, which have showers and a swimming pool, guys basically do nothing but roam the halls and have sex with one partner after another—for twelve or even twenty-four hours straight. Afterward, I'd go home and sleep for the rest of the weekend.

During several summers I went in with a bunch of guys and rented a beach house in a gay area of Fire Island, a resort just off the coast of Long Island. We'd hop the train right after work on Friday, then take a ferry across to Fire Island, where we'd have sex, drugs, and parties until late Sunday night. As I strolled the beach, gazing at all the oiled-and-tanned men's bodies in tiny bathing suits, I'd think, *This is wonderful—I must be in heaven.* I couldn't wait for the next weekend.

Running from thrill to thrill, from weekend to weekend, essentially describes what I lived for during the next seventeen years. I stayed in New York—sometimes with male lovers, sometimes alone—and established a reasonably successful career in the education field. I oversaw the adult education and community service programs for the Bronx Community College for seven years. Then I lectured and consulted in the area of fund-raising until 1981, when I joined my most recent employer, Cooperative Educational Services, in Norwalk, Connecticut.

I kept telling myself I was happy.

Actually, I experienced a range of feelings during these years, none of which approached real happiness.

For one thing, I felt terribly guilty over having left Marsha and especially Libby, who continued to live in the New York area. Marsha was angry and (understandably) bitter for some time. Though she had every right to vent those feelings and turn Libby against me, however, she chose not to. Libby adjusted to my absence with great difficulty; I kept in touch with her, but our contact was infrequent and inconsistent. I found it so hard to call or get together with her because I was immediately reminded of how deeply I had hurt her. When the guilt got too strong, I'd avoid contacting her altogether for a while.

To my amazement she never expressed anger or hostility at me, or attempted to blame me for the pain I'd caused her. I think she turned it inward, even blaming herself at times. She seemed to enjoy our rare get-togethers, and I even got the feeling that she looked up to me.

Once, when she was in second or third grade, she gave me a paper she had written, along with a picture of me she had drawn and colored. The paper said:

Why I Love My father

because he taKes me
out to dinner. because
he taKes me to art
shows. because he lets
me spend the weeKend
with him. because he
lets me have tV dinners
at his house when I
want them. because he
lets me stay up late.
because he was wonderful
when he showed my
class movies.

I absolutely loved receiving things like this, but they only reawakened my guilt, which I continually tried to bury. As she got older, I'd call her occasionally after school and offer to pick her up for dinner. If I happened to be living alone and didn't have a lover, I'd sometimes invite her to stay with me for a weekend. When Libby was in ninth grade, Marsha remarried and they moved to Washington, D.C. I saw even less of Libby then, but she still sent me cards and letters.

Guilt about Libby was the closest thing I felt to any sort of moral or spiritual sensibility. I had completely shed all evidence of Christian faith, and basically considered myself a libertarian: I believed I was free to do anything I wanted as long as it didn't hurt someone else. And I lived out this belief, such as it was, to the fullest.

From time to time Peggy would call just to keep in touch. She'd fill me in on all her kids, whom I felt close to and usually saw over the holidays. Then she'd inquire about what I was doing. Inevitably she'd ask questions like, "Tom, are you going to church anywhere?" or "Have you been reading your Bible much?" She and her kids talked to me freely about being born again, though without putting much pressure on me. I would usually pass it off without much thought. After all, I had been to Union Seminary and knew that their brand of faith was far too simple for me.

A second feeling, possibly the predominant feeling of my gay lifestyle, was loneliness. I hated being alone, and would do almost anything to avoid it. Weekends were no problem, since I spent virtually every waking moment at the discos or the baths. Weeknights I'd go out to dinner with my lover (when I had one), and then we'd watch TV together. When I didn't have a lover, however, I'd feel this aching, almost fearful sense of emptiness when I got home from work each day. I found it difficult to stay home alone—I'd have to get out and be with other men. So I'd usually run to the baths for a few hours.

Constant, compulsive social and sexual activity, I thought, would keep me from being lonely. But it didn't: even around other people, the interaction often seemed so shallow. So I resorted to drugs and alcohol to mask the void that remained in me. When I did end up home alone, I'd cope by smoking marijuana and floating off into space.

In contrast to all the superficial acquaintances I had in the gay community, three guys stood out as devoted friends: Tony, Andrew, and Will. While I never had social contact with most men outside of the bars and baths, I often got together with these guys for dinner, and a great friendship developed between us. But they were the only bright spot in an otherwise lonely existence.

A third feeling, which I experienced many times, was jealousy. It happened in every one of my lover relationships, which tended to be stormy and short-lived. Whenever I entered into a relationship, there was always the unspoken understanding that neither of us would be faithful, i.e., monogamous. It was a contradictory position for me, since I fooled around with other men all the time, yet demanded total faithfulness from my partner. As soon as I learned my lover had seen someone else, however, I'd erupt in a jealous fury that often led to nasty fistfights. Unfaithfulness affected me so strongly, I believe, because it stirred up all the childhood feelings of being rejected and ignored and unloved by my father.

Related in part to this jealousy were periods of intense anger toward my parents. At one point I sought the help of a therapist to sort out these feelings and better understand my parental upbringing. I wasn't yet open to the possibility of changing my lifestyle, but the therapist did help me begin the process of accepting my parents and letting go of some of my anger.

About this time, my relationship with my dad took a significant turn. I first noticed it during one of my annual Christmas visits with my parents. Dad seemed to be much warmer and more affectionate than in previous years. He hugged me often, and wanted to sit down and ask me questions about my job. For the first time I sensed that he genuinely cared about me and was interested in me.

He must have been going through some changes himself, because his attitude toward me took on a strikingly different tone on subsequent visits. Later he even brought up the subject of my childhood, and admitted that he had made many mistakes in the way he had raised me. He told me how sorry he was, and asked for my forgive-

ness. I felt that huge distance between my father and me—
the distance that so profoundly affected the course of my
life—beginning to lessen.

It took a few years, but I eventually came to realize
that if there was ever a time when my father didn't love
me, he did love me now. I found myself forgiving him, and
my anger at him beginning to dissipate. Our relationship
was healing in a major way.

This dramatic shift in my feelings toward my dad had
a surprising side effect—one that I didn't see the significance of until years later. For the very first time in my
life I began to feel flickers of heterosexual desire. I actually
felt attracted—sexually attracted—to a woman. This was
a whole new experience for me. We dated for a while, and I
even had satisfying sexual intercourse with her several
times before the relationship ended. Later on I got sexually
involved with another woman, which indicated to me that
these heterosexual urges I was feeling were real and not
just a curiosity.

Despite these important new developments I basically
continued my active gay lifestyle as before, without giving
myself much opportunity to reflect on the quality or
morality of my life, or whether I wanted to make any
changes in myself.

A routine visit to my doctor in 1983 changed all that.

I made a point of seeing Dr. Ron Grossman, a New
York physician, on a regular basis to make sure I hadn't
picked up any sexually transmitted diseases such as
syphilis or gonorrhea. (These infections are common
among sexually active homosexuals and heterosexuals,
and are easily treated by antibiotics.) On this particular
visit Dr. Grossman's eyes showed a sudden concern as he
looked in my mouth.

"What's wrong?" I asked.

"Tom," he said, "I'm afraid we've got a case of
thrush here."

My heart immediately sank into my stomach. I knew what thrush was. For a couple of years I had been hearing and reading about a strange, new, deadly disease called Acquired Immune Deficiency Syndrome, which at this time was striking down many homosexuals and a few heterosexuals. It attacks and breaks down the immune system, making one susceptible to a host of unusual infections that a healthy person's system naturally fends off. As the immune system deteriorates, the person eventually dies.

I had read that thrush, a fungus, was one of these unusual infections, and could signal that a person had been exposed to AIDS. (Thrush can also occur vaginally in women, especially pregnant women, and in people of either sex who have taken large dosages of antibiotics. In these cases it does not necessarily indicate exposure to AIDS, and is easily treated by a doctor.) Since I maintained such a sexually active lifestyle, I realized my case of thrush probably meant I had been exposed.

Nevertheless, I was stunned. Until now, I hadn't believed I'd actually contract this disease. AIDS was still relatively new and not very widespread; I only knew one person who had contracted it. I'd tell myself, *Tom, you're not going to get it. Look around you—nearly all your friends have been doing the same things as you, and none of them have gotten it.* Yet everything I'd read had clearly indicated that people with my kind of lifestyle had the highest risk of exposure. And that the disease had no cure.

I sat there on the examining table, speechless. Dr. Grossman tried to encourage me, but I told him I wanted to get another opinion just to be sure. He sent me to a local doctor who was participating in an AIDS study sponsored by the National Institute of Health: The doctor needed volunteers to test for helper T-cell levels in their blood. (Helper T-cells, the body's primary disease fighters, are destroyed by the AIDS virus. But since at this time the actual AIDS virus hadn't been discovered, the only way to "guess" whether someone had been exposed was to measure his helper T-cell levels. The AIDS virus itself, termed HIV for Human Immunodeficiency Virus, was first isolated in 1984.)

Sure enough, the doctor reported that my T-cell level was abnormally low. In his opinion, I had definitely been exposed to the AIDS virus, and I needed to take immediate precautions to avoid passing it on to others. He told me my condition was known as ARC, which stands for AIDS-Related Complex. It was not AIDS, but could develop into full-blown AIDS—maybe in a few months, maybe not for years, and possibly never.

I didn't want to believe him. I wanted to deny it all, just as I had been denying that my lifestyle needed changing ever since I heard about AIDS. I had lived with this idea that I was indestructible—that I could live however I wanted and that life would go on forever. But this news cast a dark shadow over all of that. Suddenly I was rudely awakened to the reality of my own mortality— my own *imminent* mortality. And I wasn't prepared. There was nothing left in my belief system to help me understand death, nothing to ease the pain of realizing that this life of mine would soon come to an end.

I slumped into a depression for several months, and began to lose my will to live. Since doctors hadn't had a lot of experience with AIDS, they couldn't give very specific predictions about my prognosis. Often I'd worry that I only had a few months left, and figured that all I could do was give up. Then I started thinking, *Since I don't have much longer to live, why not make the most of the time I have left?* So, having settled on this pessimistic twist of a beer slogan as my stopgap operating philosophy, I pretty much continued to live as promiscuously as before, except that I always used a condom.

For the next three years, I kept up my gay lifestyle without noticing any effects from the deadly virus I carried in my blood. But I did begin to notice a different kind of effect—the negative effect on my soul of seeking mere physical pleasure for so many years when what I really wanted was a deep sense of inner fulfillment. Though my fast and frenzied lifestyle still held plenty of allure, I began to acknowledge the emptiness, the shallowness, of it. I moved into a stage where sex became more of a bad habit than anything else: I knew it wasn't bringing me happiness, yet I couldn't stop, and I didn't know what else to do anyway.

The issue of my health nagged at me constantly. Some days I'd feel resigned to the fact that I would die soon; on other days I'd think that maybe if I slowed my life down, curbed my sexual activity, and ate healthy food, I'd be able to stave off the disease. In October of 1986, I even moved to an apartment in Norwalk, Connecticut—partly to be closer to my job, and partly because I thought I might be less tempted to visit the gay baths of New York. My plan worked—partly. Weekday visits stopped, but I still found myself driving into the city on weekends. During the week, I'd pour as much energy as I could into my job, and then usually spend the evenings home, alone and isolated, washing down my depression with a six-pack of beer.

Around the end of October I noticed I was feeling low-grade fevers in the mornings at work. At first I just ignored them, even though I knew they were signs of infection. Then, as they grew more frequent, I tried to dismiss them in usual Tom Stribling fashion. By the third week of November they still hadn't gone away.

One day I woke up with a fairly high fever, and was feeling very weak, but I stupidly made myself get up and go to work anyway. At the office, I was greeted by the very thing I needed on a day like that—a flood in the computer room. Quickly I obtained the use of a large, industrial vacuum cleaner that sucks up water, and attempted to operate it. I had hardly pushed it back and forth a couple of times when I felt so exhausted that I had to sit down. So I told my boss I wasn't feeling well, and I went home to bed.

After sleeping for a few hours, I woke up feeling hotter and weaker. It was finally happening to me. I phoned Dr. Grossman and said, "Well, Ron, I think this is it. I think the time has come." Then I described my symptoms to him. He wanted me to check in immediately at the emergency room of my local hospital, but I told him I was too afraid that word of my condition might get around in my town.

"Can you get into the city, then?"

"Yeah, I think so."

When I dragged myself out of bed, however, I wondered whether I'd even make it to my apartment door. Now I not only felt weak, but had severe shortness of breath. Every movement of my body took extreme effort. Taking a shower was nearly impossible because I couldn't even stand up for more than a minute at a time. I had to sit down on the toilet seat in order to dry myself off. Getting dressed proved to be equally exhausting: I put on one sock, and then had to lie back in my chair for five or ten minutes just to catch my breath. Then the other sock, and so on. It took all afternoon to get ready, get a cab to the train, and struggle into Dr. Grossman's office just before closing time.

He took me in immediately, and X-rayed my chest. My lungs were covered with a white, milky fluid. "This is a classic case of pneumocystis carinii pneumonia," he said. "It wouldn't have gotten nearly this bad if you'd called me earlier." He explained that this kind of pneumonia can be easily cleared up if it is treated with antibiotics at the low-grade fever stage.

Dammit, I scolded myself. *Why didn't I call him sooner? Then I wouldn't be so sick now.*

Dr. Grossman said I should get into a hospital right away. He called the New York University Medical Center across the street from his office, but they said there were no openings until tomorrow. So, to my dismay, I had to return home that night and repeat the exhausting task of getting myself cleaned up, dressed, on the train, and back to the hospital in New York. It took most of the next day, but I finally made it.

At the hospital, they ran a tube down into my lung and took a biopsy to confirm the diagnosis. Pneumocystis is actually a rare form of pneumonia caused by bacteria that reside in everyone's lungs. A healthy person's immune system automatically keeps the bacteria population down, but when one's immune system has been weakened—by the AIDS virus, for example—the bacteria multiply until they choke off the lungs. Doctors who work with AIDS patients know that in most cases, pneumocystis carinii pneumonia (PCP for short) signals the onslaught of fully developed AIDS.

I lay in my bed, alone and scared. I now had AIDS. I was going to die soon. I needed to call somebody, but I couldn't call anyone in my family because I didn't want them to know that I had AIDS. (They already knew I was gay.) Word would get around at the office if I tried to confide to anyone there. (I did call in sick, though, without offering any explanation.) So I called my three best friends—Andrew, Tony, and Will—and they all came to visit. Andrew even stayed in my hospital room one night. Their support and comfort meant a lot to me.

The hospital treated me with Bactrim, a strong antibiotic. Almost immediately my condition improved: the fever and shortness of breath vanished. And my appetite returned, which was important because I had lost nearly thirty pounds in those few days. I recovered so rapidly that they offered to release me after only one day, but I asked to stay for one more.

Afterward I met with Dr. Grossman in his office. "How long do I have?" I asked him.

"Well, it's hard to say," he replied. "I had one case where it was only ten months from the time he contracted PCP to the time he died of a brain infection. Statistically, though, the average is one to two years from the time of diagnosis. Since your medical history is good, and you went for nearly four years after exposure before contracting AIDS, I think you may last a little longer than the average."

Some encouragement. Dr. Grossman then gave me a few closing instructions: eat lots of protein, avoid junk food, come back for a follow-up appointment, and call him immediately if I experienced any unusual symptoms. He also arranged for me to receive free dosages of AZT, an experimental drug just approved by the Federal Drug Administration that reportedly helped to slow the progress of AIDS. The drug would be administered by the hospital dispensary each week.

I returned to work and tried to get on with life. At the office, I guessed that people suspected I might have AIDS, since I hadn't yet gained my weight back. (They already knew, but never mentioned that I was gay.) I said nothing except that I had been sick and was now feeling better. In fact, I felt so much better physically after the pneumonia that I was nearly euphoric. My weight was returning, and I had so much more energy that my spirits improved temporarily. *Maybe I've got much longer to live than I thought*, I even said to myself at one point.

But as the realization set in that I now had AIDS, my initial euphoria turned to a lonely despondency. I badly needed the love and support of my family, but couldn't bear to break the news to them. Besides Dr. Grossman, my three friends were the only ones who knew. They showed remarkable caring toward me: Andrew frequently stayed at my apartment to keep me company, and Tony checked in by phone almost daily. But they were all the support I had.

With all the hubbub over my health, Thanksgiving had

somehow passed without my even noticing. I had little to be thankful for, anyway. For all I knew, I'd be dead by next Thanksgiving. I coped with my depression by hurling myself into my job—working late, working on weekends—and by drinking heavily whenever I got home. I hardly drove into New York at all.

The forthcoming Christmas holiday began to worry me. I had already told my parents I'd visit them, but since I still hadn't gained all my weight back I feared they'd figure out I had AIDS. (Rock Hudson's death had significantly increased the public's awareness of AIDS, and I'm sure it had fueled my parents' fears.) I knew they wouldn't be able to handle it if they found out. I kept debating whether I should go.

Around this time I had a vivid dream. A clear, distinct voice said to me: "I'm going to give you till the holidays. But if you don't decide, then I'm going to choose for you." It was so vivid that I knew it was significant, but I couldn't figure out what it meant. Maybe it referred to my decision about going home for Christmas. I wondered about it for a while and then dismissed it. Little did I know just how significant that dream would turn out to be.

A few days before Christmas I realized I just couldn't go through with it. I was too afraid to go back home. So I made up an excuse and called my parents.

"Hi, Dad, what's happening out there?" I said, trying to be cheery.

"Well, at this moment I'm cutting up a pineapple for you, Tom. As soon as you get here you can have some fresh pineapple."

Wonderful.

"Uh, Dad, I'm sorry, but I have something to tell you. I'm not going to be able to come, after all. Something's come up at work, and I can't take time off right now."

He didn't get upset or anything, but I could hear the

disappointment in his voice. "Well, Tom, we understand," he said. "I know your job's important to you, so don't worry—we understand. You just have a good Christmas, okay?"

I had a lousy Christmas. Andrew came over for a while on Christmas Eve, and I bought a couple of bottles of champagne. But then he went home to be with his family, and I spent Christmas Day alone. I drank the rest of the champagne, along with quite a few beers. Between Christmas and New Year's I had to stay home because I had already arranged for the week off from work and would have to explain myself if I showed up at the office. It was kind of a lost week. I spent most of it drinking, except for visiting Tony and Will once or twice in New York. I even skipped my appointment with Dr. Grossman because I had been drinking that morning and knew he wouldn't have approved. I felt so lonely and disheartened.

On New Year's Eve and all day on New Year's Day I stayed home and got loaded. I stayed loaded for the next two days. Sometime after dinner on January 3, 1987, I said to my drunken self, *This is ridiculous. I refuse to be lonely any longer. I'm going to go find some company.* So I stumbled out of my apartment, climbed into my Cavalier, and headed for a sleazy bar I frequented in Bridgeport, about fifteen miles north of Norwalk.

The next thing I knew—sometime after midnight on January 4—a policeman had clubbed me and arrested me for running down a young woman on a Bronx expressway.

It's a measure of the Father's love for us that he allows us to persist in our own free will. And no matter how long we persist, no matter how far away from him we stray, it is a greater measure of his love that he waits with outstretched arms for that moment when we desist from our selfish ways and say, like the Prodigal Son, "Father, I want to come home."

From testimony Tom gave in Cedar Rapids, Iowa, February 1988, on the one-year anniversary of his conversion

SIX
SIX
SIX
SIX
SIX

On the forty-five-minute flight to Cedar Rapids, I put my head back in my seat and closed my eyes. I felt completely exhausted, body and soul, but I also felt a deep sense of relief. I hardly even thought about my criminal charges or my court appearance. The only thing that went through my mind was, *I'm safe, I'm safe.* I guess I really did want to live after all. I couldn't wait to get to Peggy's.

The Cedar Rapids Municipal Airport is too tiny for the moving passageways that connect the plane to the terminal, so all the passengers must get off the plane into the January freeze and walk across the runway area to reach the terminal. Once inside, I searched for Peggy's familiar face. At the end of a long hallway, I saw her standing in the waiting area with her husband, Gary, at her side.

Upon seeing me, she immediately burst into tears. They both threw their arms around me and I began to cry as well. They were glad to see me—even after all I had done. That was hard for me to fathom.

Not much was said during the car ride back to her house. Gary, who is by nature a quiet guy, drove in silence while Peggy made small talk. For a few minutes the smell of oatmeal filled the air as we passed the huge Quaker Oats plant. Peggy briefly mentioned how she had found out about my disappearance, and that Jerry had called Mom and Dad. At this point I didn't really care who knew about me. I just felt relieved and safe. I felt that I was going home.

When I took off my coat at the house, Peggy looked at me and said, in a big-sisterly way, "You look a mess. And your skin is pale." (No wonder: I had eaten hardly a thing in the past two weeks, and I had already lost weight from my bout with pneumonia.)

Then she saw the dried blood on my shirt cuffs. "Tom, what have you done to yourself?" she said gently, pulling up my sleeves. "Those cuts are going to need stitches."

I said I'd rather not go to a hospital because they might lock me up in a psych ward or something. Besides, I was still a little paranoid about being discovered and reported to the police.

"Well, let me at least call the hospital and ask their advice." They told her that their normal procedure in the event of a suicide attempt is to give a psychological examination, and depending on the results, either hospitalize the patient in the psych unit or release him. Just what I thought.

"Let's forget the hospital," I said. "I can live with these scars."

"Well, okay," Peggy conceded. "But let me clean them up at least." I followed her into the bathroom, where she calmly proceeded to dab my wounds with cotton balls dipped in hydrogen peroxide. The procedure stung.

As we stood there in front of the sink, I noticed that my wrists were bleeding a little; Peggy had opened up a few of the cuts while cleaning them. Suddenly it occurred to me that my blood was infected. I hadn't been thinking about the fact that I had AIDS.

"Wait, Peggy," I said, pulling my arms away. "You'd better let me do this."

Without a moment's hesitation, she replied, "No, it's okay—I'm not afraid." It was a simple, direct answer, probably given without a thought. Peggy knew I had AIDS. Yet there was no question in her mind that she was going to cleanse my wounds.

Something in me stirred as Peggy continued quietly and calmly to wipe the blood from my wrists. My heart, which for so long had been cold, hard, and afraid, was beginning to break. Yes, I was relieved to be alive and with my family, but until this moment I hadn't experienced anything close to a change of heart.

I'm not afraid. Such simple words from Peggy, yet they meant so much. What I heard, in my heart, was more than her lack of fear. What my heart heard was, *I have no reason to be afraid, Tom, because I'm only doing what Christ would have done. I'm loving my brother as Christ loved me.* Those words came through so clearly that I almost thought Peggy had actually said them.

She finished cleaning me up, and carefully bandaged my wrists. Several times she said, "Tom, I'm afraid you're going to have terrible scars." But I didn't care. I was just glad to be there, and glad to be alive. I went into the living room and plopped onto the sofa. Gary and Peggy joined me.

Figuring that they at least deserved some kind of explanation for my behavior, I briefly described how I had been arrested and thrown in jail for a hit-and-run accident I couldn't remember, and that instead of spending the rest of my short life in jail, I had decided to kill myself. I explained how I had traveled from city to city, trying to build up the nerve to go through with it, and had ended up in Chicago.

"Well, you have a lawyer now, Tom," Peggy said. "His name is Lee Ahlers, and he told me to tell you not to worry. Your case has been to court and the judge has issued a bench warrant for your arrest. A bench warrant just sits on the judge's desk. Nobody will be looking for you as long as you agree to go back. Your lawyer said you shouldn't have anything to worry about."

Then she added, "The folks know. Of course they're having a hard time, but Pastor Steve [Peggy's pastor] has been in touch with Dad several times to encourage him and pray with him. And I called to let them know you were on your way here from Chicago."

I didn't know what to say. I wondered how Peggy knew so much about my case, and how I had a lawyer when I had never arranged for one. She must have told my parents herself. I had this feeling that a lot had been going on since that first day I had stepped on the plane for New Orleans.

Peggy continued. Normally she works during the day, but she had developed a case of strep throat and had stayed home for several days. One of those days was when she had received my first desperate phone call. After I had hung up on her, she sprang into action, calling Jerry and my other sister, Paula, Mom and Dad, B.J. in New York, and Steve, her pastor.

In addition, Peggy and B.J. had prayed for me over the phone each day since I called. She had also been meeting two women over at the church early each morning to pray. These people in turn had told others to pray for me, she explained, so that there were people all over the country asking God to protect me. All of this love and concern and prayer on my account astonished me; my heart broke even more. Why would all these people worry about me?

Then Peggy told me about Jerry. "Jerry's the one who called the lawyer and made all the arrangements. He got the lawyer's name from B.J., and sent him money for a retainer fee." Jerry, who wouldn't give me a dime earlier, had gone to all that trouble over me? Upon hearing this, my heart broke wide open. I felt as if a door had opened in my chest, and love was pouring in—Jerry's love, my folks' love, Peggy's love, the love of all those who had prayed for me. I was overwhelmed.

Finally Peggy said, "It'd probably be good for you to give the folks and Jerry a call." I dialed Jerry's number first, since my greatest anxiety was over my legal situation.

"Oh, Tom—I'm so happy to hear you!" he said in a warm voice. He sounded like my brother who loved me.

"Jerry, I heard what you did for me and I want you to know how much I appreciate it. And I want to be sure you understand that I didn't try to commit suicide because you turned me down for money."

"I didn't think it was," he assured me. "Want to know something? You don't realize how many people there are in New York who love you."

"What do you mean?" I said.

He went on to tell me how he had called B.J. and had gotten Lee Ahlers' phone number. "I'll be glad to help Tom when he returns to New York," Lee had told Jerry, "but there's really nothing more I can do right now since I don't know any of the facts of the case."

After talking with Lee, Jerry had also called my friend Tony, who a few weeks before had angrily told Jerry over the phone that I had AIDS. When Tony heard what the lawyer had said, he had called Lee himself and said, "What are you doing for Tom?"

"There's nothing I can do—I know nothing about his case," Lee must have said.

Hot under the collar, Tony had retorted, "What do you mean you can't do anything? You're a lawyer!"

Lee had explained to Tony that he didn't know which part of the court my case was in, so he couldn't locate my judge or my case number. So Tony had gotten on the phone himself, called the courthouse several times, and tracked down my case number and which judge had been assigned to me. Then he had called Lee back and given him all the information. Jerry had then followed up by sending Lee a one-thousand-dollar retainer fee.

As Jerry told me all of this, I could hardly believe my

ears. Such concern and care and love from my brother and from Tony—all on my account. But there was more.

Jerry had also spoken to my landlord in Connecticut, because my other friend Andrew had come by looking for me and found an eviction notice on my door. (In my state of depression I had fallen two months behind in my rent.) Andrew had notified Jerry, who in turn contacted my landlord and told him I was having personal problems. My landlord had replied, "Well, if Tom's having problems right now, don't worry about it. Just send me one month's rent and we'll call it even until he gets back." So Jerry had sent him a check to cover my rent.

"I couldn't believe it," Jerry said as he ended his story. "Even your landlord loves you. You're the most loved person in New York!"

As I hung up the phone, I basked in those words. I was *loved*. My conversation with Jerry only added to the outpouring of love I was feeling from my family and friends. It was the very thing I needed.

Next, I knew I had to call my parents. Nervously I dialed their number at the trailer park in Texas, where they live for the winter.

"Dad?"

He recognized my voice instantly. "Hallelujah, praise the Lord!" he exclaimed, bursting into tears. "The prodigal son has returned!"

"Dad—" I said through my tears, "I just wish you were here to throw your arms around me."

"They *are* around you," he said softly.

We didn't talk long. Dad closed by saying, "Now, Tom, don't you worry. God's going to bring you through this. You just keep your faith." Funny he would say that, I thought, since I hadn't professed any faith in twenty years. But I had to admit that God was somehow involved in what had happened to me today.

By now it was late at night, and I wanted to go to bed.

My two phone calls had left me feeling happy but utterly drained emotionally. Peggy urged me to make one more call. "You've got to call Libby," she said. "She's waiting up for you."

Libby, the one I'd abandoned to follow my homosexual desires. Libby, the one I'd almost abandoned again by trying to kill myself. I wanted to let her know I was all right, but I didn't think I could face her just this moment. It would be too hard.

"Peggy," I said, "I just don't think I can handle it tonight. Could you call her for me and tell her I'm so exhausted that I went to bed, and let her know that I'll call her first thing in the morning?" Peggy said okay, she would. Then I collapsed into bed. Only twenty-four hours earlier I had been slicing my wrists in that shabby Chicago hotel room, yet those hours seemed like weeks. So much had happened.

"Tom? Tom, wake up." It was Peggy's voice, and her hand on my shoulder. "Tom, it's seven o'clock, and you need to call Libby now because her first class is at seven-thirty. She said for you to be sure and call her before seven-thirty."

I sat up in bed and tried to collect my thoughts. It was hard enough to call Jerry and Dad, but I found it far more difficult to muster the nerve to phone Libby. She was my daughter; she looked up to me. I was supposed to be an example to her. What could I say to her now? How could I explain what I was going through? I hadn't yet told her that I had AIDS, and she knew nothing about the accident.

Right away she picked up the phone. "Dad?" Her voice was so precious, and yet so anxious. We both dissolved into tears. I had caused her so much pain; she didn't deserve all that I had put her through. All I could say to her was, "Honey, I'm sorry. I'm so sorry." I didn't know how she'd respond; she had every right to be furious with me.

"Dad," she said, sniffling, "You don't have to explain anything to me. You just have to know that I love you, and don't you ever forget it."

She may never know how deeply her words touched me. It had broken my heart to know I was loved and accepted by my parents, and by Peggy and Jerry. But to hear those words from the lips of my own daughter awakened something in my soul. I began to feel ashamed of all I had done over the past twenty years—not just to Libby, but to my whole family, to myself . . . even to God.

The call was brief; Libby had to get to class. I carried these thoughts with me into the kitchen, where Peggy was fixing me a bowl of oatmeal and wheat toast. I sat down and ate a little, mostly in silence; I wanted to figure out just what I was feeling. The message that God loved me was already coming through loud and clear. I realized he was loving me through Peggy, through Jerry, through my parents, through Libby. God loved me so much that he had grabbed me by the scruff of the neck and yanked me out of the jaws of death.

But now, after my conversation with Libby, I was feeling something more. I wanted to tell God I was sorry. Something in me moved, and I found myself turning to Peggy, who was nonchalantly cleaning up the kitchen.

"Peggy, would you pray with me?" I heard myself say.

"Of course I would, Tom," she said, smiling softly. Maybe she knew what was going on in my soul. Or maybe she could tell my heart was breaking last night when I heard how many people had been praying for me, caring for me, trying to help me. Perhaps it was just that simple, inner belief that she's always had about me since she committed her own life to Christ.

She sat down next to me and said, "Tom, it's a very simple prayer. Just ask God to forgive you, and ask Jesus to be the master of your life." Simple, I thought. The very thing I've detested about Peggy's faith for all these years. It had always seemed too simple, but no longer. Now it made perfect sense.

So I knelt on the floor, bowed my head, and prayed that simple prayer.

I was totally unprepared for what I saw when I looked up at Peggy. To my amazement, her face radiated with joy and light. A luminescent glow seemed to surround her. I felt that I was experiencing a vision—an image of my heavenly Father looking upon me, his hands open, saying, "Welcome home, Tom."

Overcome with emotion, I began to cry. Peggy held me and we sobbed together for the next few minutes. For the first time in my life, I felt truly free—free from within. I felt forgiven. I felt alive.

While I sat there at the table, trying to take in what had just happened to me, Peggy went to call her pastor. "Steve," she said excitedly, "Guess what—we have a new entrant into the kingdom of God!" I didn't talk to him just then, but I agreed to let him visit me that afternoon. In the meantime, I had a couple of other calls to make. First, I called Dad and told him I had just committed my life to Christ. Again, tears of joy flowed for most of the call.

Next, Peggy suggested that I phone my lawyer, Lee Ahlers, in New York. "He's a Christian," she said, "and we've prayed for you over the phone several times. He'll be delighted to hear what you've just done." Since I had never met Lee before, and I was still anxious about the status of my case, I agreed to call.

"Lee, I want you to know that something wonderful has happened to me." I gave a brief explanation of the past two days. "Praise the Lord!" he kept saying.

The conversation then turned to my legal situation. "When should I come back to New York?" I asked him.

"Well, how do you feel?"

"Pretty exhausted."

"Then why don't you just stay there for a week and rest. Give yourself some time to recover. I'll get back in touch with the district attorney and set a new court date. He's already told me that he won't do anything until you come back." At least I had some time to recuperate.

Peggy also called B.J. and told him the news. He was thrilled, and when I got on the phone with him, he told me to be sure to contact him when I got back to New York. I checked in with my boss to let him know I was okay and that I'd be back to work the following week. He seemed pretty understanding, and told me to call in when I returned.

That afternoon I relaxed in the warmth, security, and love of Peggy and Gary's home. My niece Cynthia, Peggy's oldest daughter, came over and threw her arms around me. She, too, had been praying for me, and told me how glad she was that I was okay. She was even more thrilled to learn of my new beginning with God.

As I waited for Pastor Steve to arrive, I reflected a bit more on what had happened that morning. Though it had been an incredibly powerful experience, only a few hours later I couldn't honestly say that I felt all that different. I wondered if maybe I had just been carried away on a climactic wave of emotion. After all, it had been a very stressful two weeks.

I voiced my doubts to Peggy. I told her I thought when someone "got saved," there was a zap and suddenly everything would change. "How can I know that what happened is real, genuine?" I asked.

"Tom, I *know* it was genuine," she reassured me. "I felt it. I know God heard that prayer."

Still, I wondered why I didn't feel any different. After all, I had already committed my life to God once, at age ten—or so I thought. That experience didn't seem to "take." At that time my homosexual desires hadn't gone away, even as I had pleaded with God to make them disappear. Who's to say that my renewed commitment now would bring about real change in my life?

So when Pastor Steve, a friendly young man with prematurely gray hair, came over, I asked him the same question I had asked Peggy. He explained that it's natural to have doubts, especially at the beginning. As I spent time reading the Bible and getting to know God better, he said, I'd feel more sure that what I did this morning was real. Sometimes that assurance doesn't come immediately, he added. It may be more of a gradual thing.

Before he left, he suggested I read the Gospel of John and the book of Romans from the New Testament. Twenty years ago I had not only read those books, I had preached on them. Those ancient words (and probably my sermons, too) had seemed pretty hollow then. I wondered how they would sound to me now.

For the next week I rested and read my Bible. Peggy's strep had cleared up, so she went back to work, leaving me at home alone. Cynthia and her sister Marla stopped by often, their cute little kids in tow, to check on me.

I had a few good hours each day with the Scriptures. To my surprise, they came alive before my very eyes. I could hardly believe that these were the same words I had analyzed and dissected in seminary—all the while missing out on the deep truth they were telling. Now, these words of Jesus and Paul leaped off the pages and cut to my heart. Even when I turned to the Old Testament book of Isaiah, the prophecies about Jesus rang with truth and authority.

At times I would pause from my reading and wonder again: Is all of this real? Should I pinch myself to make sure I'm awake instead of dreaming this? I knew my spirit had been awakened in some way, perhaps for the first time in my life. And it felt wonderful. Why fight it? But there was still the other part of me that questioned the experience and tried to write it off as an emotional high. I decided to take Pastor Steve's advice and continue giving myself time with God and with the Bible.

While I've heard stories of people who claimed their lives changed instantaneously the day they turned to Christ, I don't think this was true for me. My conversion felt like more of a beginning—a starting point—a door that had opened in my soul. During my week of reading Scripture and being quiet before God, however, I did feel two strong convictions almost immediately.

The first was that I believed the Bible to be the inspired Word of God. I had never believed that before, even while studying at Union Theological Seminary to become a minister. There I was taught to view the Bible primarily as a historical, literary document. I could analyze, critique, and interpret it just as I would any ancient text, but I wasn't necessarily taught that the entire Scriptures were inspired by God and fully authoritative.

The second conviction was about the promiscuous homosexual lifestyle I had been living. Until now I had rationalized my sexual orientation as something I must have been born with and couldn't do anything about. I had thought I had no choice but to follow after my desires and pursue sexual relationships with other men. I had gone even beyond this to the point that I just went after raw, anonymous sex.

Now I was feeling a clear sense that my lifestyle had been displeasing to God. At this point I didn't know any more than that. I hadn't sorted out any of the theological questions about homosexuality, or even come to the position that homosexuality was always wrong for everyone. I just knew in my own self that I had dishonored God by my promiscuous lifestyle.

My week of rest and recuperation passed far too quickly. All week I had been surrounded by love and support and comfort. I attended church with Peggy and Gary on Sunday, and went out to dinner with them another evening. My nieces and nephews and their kids flowed in and out of the house, always wanting to be with their Uncle Tom. Now that it was time for me to return to New York, I didn't want to leave. Peggy's home was such a safe place. Even though I'd only visited there a few times, it felt like home to me. I wanted to stay.

Besides, I worried about all that I had to face when I got back: my upcoming court appearance, my boss at work, and my doctor, for starters. I had to meet with my lawyer and prepare myself for the New York City court system. I would have to explain again to my boss why I had missed nearly three more weeks of work. And then I had to figure out what to do with this new faith I had found. What would I say to my gay friends? Where would I go to church? I looked forward to meeting all the people who had prayed for me and acted on my behalf, but I still felt nervous about what direction my new relationship with God would take me. It seemed so much easier just to stay right here in Cedar Rapids, away from all that tension and pressure.

But I knew I had to return. On Saturday Peggy and Cynthia drove me to the airport. For most of the ride I sat in silence. They both knew how scared I was and that I didn't want to leave. As we neared the airport parking lot, Cynthia reached out from the back seat and put her hand on my shoulder.

"Uncle Tom," she said, "there's this passage of Scripture I always repeat to myself when I'm afraid."

"What is it?" I said.

She recited it to me from memory: " 'Do not fear, for I am with you; do not be dismayed, for I am your God. I will strengthen you and help you; I will uphold you with my righteous right hand' (Isaiah 41:10)."

That verse hit home. That was the kind of God I wanted and needed, especially now. I wanted to remember that passage.

"Could you say that again?" I asked Cynthia.

"Okay," she said, "I'll help you memorize it." There in the parking lot, we went over the verse, phrase by phrase, until I finally had it memorized. Things would be difficult back in New York. I was still afraid. But I was no longer alone. God would be with me, and he would strengthen me, help me, and uphold me. I whispered the verse to myself several more times as I boarded my plane.

*F*earing the pain involved, almost all of us, to a greater or lesser degree, attempt to avoid problems. We procrastinate, hoping that they will go away. We ignore them, forget them, pretend they do not exist. We even take drugs to assist us in ignoring them, so that by deadening ourselves to the pain we can forget the problems that cause the pain. We attempt to skirt around the problems rather than meet them head on. We attempt to get out of them rather than suffer through them.

From *The Road Less Traveled*, by M. Scott Peck

SEVEN
SEVEN
SEVEN
SEVEN
SEVEN

Once again I found myself sitting on an airplane, worrying about what would happen to me after I landed. I had been in this position several times over the past few weeks. But this flight was different. For one thing, I was flying toward my problems instead of away from them. Up to this point all I had done was ignore or avoid my problems in any way I could. Or I would try to numb the emotional pain with alcohol and Valium. Now I had decided to face these problems, and, with God's help, make the best of them. My week and a half at Peggy's and my renewed relationship with God had given me hope. I was still afraid, but I had a growing sense that things would somehow work out.

After experiencing such an outpouring of love from so many people at Peggy's, I couldn't bring myself to return to my lonely Connecticut apartment. I still needed to be around people who, I knew, cared about me, so I had arranged to stay at Tony's place in Soho for a few days. He told me he had invited my other friends Will and Andrew over for dinner. We could all eat together and get caught up on what had happened to me.

Andrew greeted me warmly at the LaGuardia Airport terminal, as did Tony and Will when we stepped into Tony's apartment. They all seemed so glad to see me and so elated that I was alive. Maybe Jerry had been right on the phone—even my friends in New York loved me.

It took me a while to finish my dinner because they wanted to know everything. I decided to tell it to them straight, just as it had happened. They listened intently. When I explained how I had renewed my commitment to Christ, they each responded differently but respectfully. Andrew kept pretty quiet. Tony said lightheartedly, "Oh, no—now we have a born-again Christian among us. What are we gonna do?"

But I knew he was taking me seriously. In fact, I sensed that all three of them had gone through their share of emotional turmoil after they found out I had disappeared. During my absence all three of them had been on the phone with Jerry, my lawyer, B.J., or each other, trying to find me or get help in handling my legal situation. These were three pretty special guys. Even the fact that my views on homosexuality were changing didn't seem to affect their concern for me.

I had a lot to do between Saturday night and my court appearance Wednesday morning. I called Lee Ahlers right after dinner to find out what arrangements we had to make. He invited me to attend St. George's Episcopal Church with him the next morning. I knew where the stately old church was—just north of Soho on 16th Street on the East Side. I had walked by it hundreds of times, but had never gone inside. It was a very established parish, heavily endowed by the Fords and the Vanderbilts. I envisioned a mostly empty sanctuary occupied by a few scattered elderly women. I have to admit, however, that I worried more about meeting Lee and getting filled in on my case than I did about the church.

He was waiting for me on the front steps. He was dressed in a three-piece suit. He had short, blondish hair, a matching mustache, and a warm face. Without saying a whole lot to me other than a friendly greeting, he led me right in and we sat down in one of the pews. Looking around, I noticed plenty of elderly women, but I also saw a large number of young professionals. Some of the people lifted their hands in the air during the service, just as some did at Peggy's church. The priest appeared to be charismatic.

Other than noticing these things, I didn't pay much attention that morning. I was fretting about what would happen with my case and I desperately wanted Lee to talk with me and reassure me. I tried to relax, telling myself that Lee would probably take me out to lunch afterward and go over all the details with me. When the liturgy ended, however, Lee told me to go downstairs for the coffee hour. So I followed him down to a room buzzing with parishioners. Soon he wandered away, which only added to my frustration.

Before long people started coming up to me. "Hi," they said, "Lee told us you were new and that we should introduce ourselves." They were friendly, but I could tell they knew nothing about me.

"How do you know Lee?" several of them asked.

"He's my lawyer," I said, not wanting to reveal much about myself. "He's representing me in a case."

I know Lee just wanted me to meet some people, but what I needed most right then was to talk with him. Finally he noticed how anxious I looked, standing there with my cup of cold coffee, and suggested we go back upstairs. We sat down in a pew in the now-empty sanctuary, and he began to catch me up on the case.

My suspicions about New York State's cracking down on drunk drivers were correct. The district attorney and (understandably) the family of the girl I hit were very angry and wanted to prosecute me in a big way, Lee said. "I don't have any idea about the DA's plan of action," he told me, "but at the very least they're going to ask for more bail money—a lot more."

This worried me. I had to borrow money to make my first bail, and I had virtually nó remaining assets. How could I possibly handle another giant bond? And if I couldn't come up with the money, what would happen to me?

"Am I going to have to go back to jail?" I asked, voicing my greatest fear.

Lee said that he had reviewed my case with two friends of his who happened to be among the best criminal lawyers in the city. Apparently they knew enough about the local court system to say that most judges don't incarcerate people with AIDS. "I can almost guarantee that you won't be going back to jail," Lee said.

You won't be going back to jail. It was just what I needed to hear. I relaxed a little as Lee went on to explain how I should prepare for Wednesday's court appearance. Though I knew I had an uphill battle ahead, I felt relieved as I left the church and walked through the rain back to Tony's.

The feeling didn't last long, however. Monday morning when I called in to my office, I was told, much to my alarm, that they were still discussing whether I would be allowed to return to my job. I knew I had been delinquent, and fully expected a reprimand and loss of a few weeks' pay. But I never thought I'd be fired. Then I was told they had found out I had AIDS. Apparently this news made them further question my job status. "We don't know if you still have a job here or not," I was told. "Don't come in until we call you."

During the next few days Tony noticed how nervous and preoccupied I was, and suggested I take a few Valiums to calm down. His offer was tempting; Valium had "helped" me through plenty of bad days before. But something in me—in the "new" me—resisted. *No, I'm not going to break down and numb myself,* I kept thinking. *I'm going to get through this with God's help.*

In lieu of tranquilizers I spent time praying and reading the Bible. Peggy helped, too, by calling me at

Tony's every day to see how I was. I told her how afraid I was about my legal mess.

"Tom, it's going to work out," she assured me. "God is using this time. He's building you, testing you. You're going to grow through this. It may take a while, but God's going to work it out according to his plan." She said that to me over and over, and I felt encouraged.

My dad also sent me a warm, supportive letter. He and my mother had prayed especially for me on the very day he wrote, asking God to give me his guidance in the days ahead. He said they were proud of me, and happy at my new beginning. "When the devil tries to get you discouraged," he wrote, "tell him you have the victory in someone who is more powerful than he is." He told me to search out every possible resource to keep control of my life, and especially to look to the Bible to strengthen my faith, and make its covenants my own. He assured me that the whole family loved me and was behind me, and "will be so happy about your new experience with the Lord. . . . Much Love, Dad."

Amid my worries about court I still delighted in my renewed relationship to God. Later Monday I stopped by B.J.'s office to tell him how I was doing. (I had already talked to him once on the phone before I left Cedar Rapids.) He seemed much different from the last time I had seen him. He sported a big smile and threw his arms around me, obviously glad to see me.

Before I had a chance to say much, B.J. asked another man, Peter Bradley, to join us in his office. He happened to be the former president of McGraw-Hill, a large New York publisher, who had recently become a Christian and left his company to pursue Christian service. The three of us sat down, and I told them my story. They were elated to hear how Christ had miraculously taken hold of me.

"God's grace was certainly at work in your life," B.J.

said. "He *wanted* to save you, brother." We prayed together, asking God to strengthen my faith and uphold me through the legal proceedings. Before I left, B.J. invited me to a men's Bible study he leads on Thursday morning—the day after my first court appearance. I told him I'd come.

I spoke with Lee several times before Wednesday. I wanted to know more about the girl I'd hit and how she was doing. Her name was Olivia, and she lived with her mother in the Chicago area. (Her parents were divorced.) She had been attending college there in Illinois, and planned to pursue a dance career. Olivia's father lived in New York, and she had been visiting him for the holidays. The accident had shattered her hip and one of her legs. (The cop's earlier report that her legs were severed had been exaggerated.) She had been confined to the hospital for reconstructive surgery and would remain there for some time. At this point, the doctors still weren't sure they could save her leg, and even if they did, they doubted she'd ever walk again.

The news about Olivia left me stricken with guilt and grief. I was totally responsible for what had happened to her. She had done nothing to bring this misfortune upon herself. Here she was, a young college student with her whole adult life and a promising career as a dancer in front of her. Now, all because of me, her life would never be the same. I asked Lee if I could visit her in the hospital, at least to tell her in person I was sorry, and show her I cared. Lee empathized with me, but said that because of the criminal charges and because there would probably be further litigation, it was best for me not to visit Olivia.

Lee went on to explain what would happen in court on Wednesday. We would be appearing before an administrative judge, who decides whether to dismiss a case or send it to another judge for a trial. If he chooses to send it on, a judge's name is drawn at random from a barrel, and the case is assigned to that judge.

Our administrative judge, Burton Roberts, has a reputation for being tough but fair, Lee told me. He tends to rule independently rather than automatically follow the wishes of the district attorney's office. "Since the DA is so adamant that you go back to jail," Lee said, "we may have something going in our favor since Roberts won't always do what the DA wants. We're lucky we have him as our presiding judge."

Lee had set up two appointments for me to help him prepare his argument to the judge. First, I went to Dr. Grossman and obtained a letter describing my medical condition and prognosis. Second, I visited a psychiatrist for a two-hour evaluation.

Wednesday morning, my alarm went off, and I sat up in bed. The court time was scheduled for 9:30 A.M.; I didn't want to be late. Tony had already gone to work, but I noticed he had left a ten-milligram Valium on the nightstand next to me. Today would be a difficult day—a tense, stressful day. My case could go to trial. I could get slapped with an exorbitant bail increase. I might have to face the parents of that poor girl I had hit, not to mention a fiery district attorney. Maybe I'd still end up in jail. I stood up and looked hard at that Valium. Maybe it would help me, just today.

No, I said to myself, and went to take a shower.

Then I came back into the room to get dressed, and stared at the Valium again. One day wouldn't hurt. I've had to go through enough stress already. It would be okay.

Once again a sense of determination rose within me, an inner strength that only God could have given me. *No, I'm not going to take it*, I repeated to myself, and walked out of the room.

I boarded the subway early so that I'd have plenty of time to find the Bronx State Supreme Court building. It was an immense, monumental structure, with an imposing flight of stone stairs leading up to it. Standing at the bottom, I felt small and helpless.

Then I remembered the Isaiah 41:10 passage Cynthia had taught me back in Cedar Rapids: "Do not fear, for I am with you; do not be dismayed, for I am your God. I will strengthen you and help you; I will uphold you with my righteous right hand." I repeated the verse over and over as I made my way up the courthouse stairs. Amazingly, by the time I reached the top, a wave of peace had washed over me. I felt safe. God would indeed uphold me even if I had to go to jail.

I located the courtroom and went inside. It looked old, with dark oak woodwork and heavy pew-like seating that faced a large, elevated judge's bench. Lee, who had arrived early, was hustling around with legal papers and talking to someone who turned out to be the DA's supervisor. Glancing around the room, I noticed a stylishly dressed woman sitting in back who, I guessed, was Olivia's mother. She appeared to be in her late thirties or early forties, and had blond hair. She also looked distraught. I was feeling mortified enough over what I had done to Olivia; I could hardly imagine how she must be feeling.

Apparently the DA's supervisor had shown up because the DA was going to be late. He didn't look very friendly, and spoke to Lee in a hurried, antagonistic tone. As I drew closer and sat down on one of the benches, I could hear some of their conversation.

". . . you know, Mr. Stribling could get depressed again," he said to Lee. "He could get inebriated again. He could get back in that car and this time he could actually kill somebody. He's tried to commit suicide. We just don't think he's a safe risk. The family of the girl he hit is very, very bitter. We think he belongs back in jail."

Lee tried to keep cool as the supervisor spouted off, but I could tell he was nervous. He doesn't usually handle criminal cases, but took a special interest in helping me when he heard about my situation and my conversion. Now he was feeling the heat.

I motioned to Lee so that he'd know I was present, and he came up to me. "Lee," I said, "there's a Scripture passage my niece gave me that has really helped me. Maybe it'll help you right now."

"Really? What is it?" As I recited the verse, his eyes lit up. He pulled out a note pad and scribbled down the reference.

"Thanks."

My case was about to be called. An assistant DA was actually handling it, but the DA himself (or his supervisor) had wanted to be present. From the corner of my eye, I saw Olivia's mother move to the front of the courtroom. She leaned forward on her bench so she could hear everything that was said. Judge Roberts, who was familiar with the case and knew I had skipped out on my last scheduled appearance, reviewed a few papers and then said to the DA's supervisor, "Now this is a voluntary return, isn't it?"

"That is correct, Your Honor," the supervisor replied.

"Well, get him up here," the judge said. "Where has he been? Why hasn't he been in court?"

At that moment the DA walked in. He apologized for being late, and then spoke briefly with his supervisor. I barely picked up the supervisor's last words: "We've got to get this guy in jail. Do your best." Then the supervisor left.

Lee asked the judge if he could approach the bench. He and the assistant DA stepped forward, and Lee handed the judge two letters—one from Dr. Grossman, and the other from the psychiatrist I had visited. Grossman's letter explained my physical condition, how he had learned of my suicide attempt, and urged the court not to incarcerate me because I needed to be free for treatment. The psychiatrist's letter described more of my personal history, suggested that the accident and my suicide attempt resulted from a sequence of extremely stressful events, and indicated that I was not likely to repeat my actions. Lee hoped the letters would show that even though I had made a serious mistake and injured an innocent young woman, I was certainly not a criminal and posed no danger to society. I would die in a year or two anyway—why spend that time in jail at a much greater cost to taxpayers?

Judge Roberts took a few minutes to read each letter carefully. The assistant DA, not wanting the defense to pull too many of the judge's heartstrings, kept trying to interrupt his reading. "Your Honor, Your Honor—we have a very serious injury here," he interjected. "A young woman who wanted to be a dancer has suffered permanent injury, may never walk again and may, in fact, lose a leg. This is an extremely serious situation, and the State is asking that Mr. Stribling be returned to jail."

"Hold off, hold off—and let me read these letters," retorted the judge. I could tell he was taking them seriously. In the few minutes I had spent before him, I felt a lot of respect for Burton Roberts. He was in his late fifties or early sixties, with gray hair. He was a bit abrasive—as many New York lawyers seem to be—but had a strong personality. He knew his mind and spoke without waffling.

When he had finished reading, he put the letters down, sat back in his chair, and took off his glasses. Then he spoke.

"I have been on the bench for many years, and have heard many tragic stories in my day," he said, "but I believe this ranks up there in the top ten most tragic of all. We have this young woman who wanted to be a dancer. She has serious injuries—there is no doubt about it. Then we have this man who is terminally ill. He tried to take his life.

"You know," he continued, "sometimes I think these

kinds of accidents—driving while intoxicated and causing personal injury—are worse than premeditated murder. But in this case, because of the great tragedy on both sides, I strongly urge that the DA and Mr. Stribling's lawyer get together immediately and work out a plea bargain. Don't come back to me until you've done that."

I didn't know exactly what the judge meant, but I figured it was good since he didn't reach into his bin and assign my case to another judge. But we weren't finished yet; there was still the matter of bail. The DA was pushing to increase my bail to a whopping fifty thousand dollars. Lee had already prepared me for that possibility, and Jerry had even sent another thousand dollars—all he could afford—to Lee's account.

Then the judge said, "Bail will stay at twenty-five hundred dollars and this case is remanded over to two weeks from now." He tapped his gavel, got up, and walked off the bench.

I breathed a sigh of relief. I had no more bail to pay, and from what I could tell, Judge Roberts was trying to keep my case from going to a trial. Apparently, he wanted the DA and Lee to work it out on their own and then come back to him with an agreement. A plea bargain, Lee explained to me, is that I would agree to plead guilty to lesser charges in exchange for the DA's dropping the more severe ones. In other words, the judge's initial ruling, while not letting me off the hook, worked to my benefit.

The assistant DA knew it, and he was hopping on the courtroom floor in anger. He rushed up to the judge as he headed for his chambers, loudly protesting that the family was furious and would never submit to a plea bargain. Not to be moved, the judge shot back: "I don't care what your problems are with the family. I don't care—that's your problem. Stall them, delay them, do whatever you have to, but I'm not going to listen to you now."

The DA and his assistant stormed out of the courtroom. Lee followed them out, hoping to discuss a plea bargain immediately. Someone from the DA's office sat down with Olivia's mother, comforting her and asking how her daughter was doing. As I stood to follow Lee out into the hall, I saw Andrew sitting in the back of the room. He had come to provide moral support.

Out in the hallway Lee was trying unsuccessfully to talk with the DA and his assistant; they kept putting him off. Then he spoke with another lawyer who had been present during the court proceedings. Lee had warned me that the family would retain a lawyer who would probably file a personal injury lawsuit in addition to the criminal charges; I realized that this man was probably that lawyer. I watched from a distance down the hallway as he chatted with Lee. Then he turned and came over to me.

He introduced himself and shook my hand. He treated me with courtesy and respect; I didn't feel threatened. "Officially I shouldn't be talking to you," he said, "but it's okay if we keep it brief. I have a summons for you, and your lawyer has indicated that you would be willing to accept it."

I said I would, and pulled out my pen to sign for it. When I saw the amount of money they wanted, I had to catch my breath: five million in compensatory damages, and another five million in punitive damages. *Maybe if I say something to this lawyer*, I thought, *he would see how upset I am over what happened and would communicate my remorse to the family.*

"Believe me," I told him, "you don't know how bad I feel about this. I have a daughter myself who is almost the same age as Olivia, and I'd feel absolutely terrible if this had happened to her."

He listened to me, and then said, "I'll be glad to relay that to the family, but I don't know if it will have any effect on them at this point. Olivia's mother is very bitter, and right now she's in the courtroom describing the extent of

Olivia's injuries in gruesome detail to the DA's assistant. They are all very, very angry."

Then he asked me if I had any assets from which I could pay damages. I said I had nothing but a life insurance policy.

At that point Olivia's mother emerged from the courtroom, and the lawyer went over to speak with her. Afraid to look directly at her, I turned away and found Lee. Despite the DA's refusal to cooperate, Lee felt quite positive about the morning's events.

"Let's find a corner someplace where we can thank God for what happened here this morning," he said. So I got Andrew, and the three of us put our arms around each other and Lee offered a prayer of thanksgiving. Then he said, "I'm going to hang around for a while and try to talk to the DA again. You guys can leave. Just be sure you don't get on the elevator with the mother. Take the stairs instead."

After the court proceedings I had to get to Dr. Grossman's office for another checkup. On the way I stopped and called Jerry to let him know the outcome. He was delighted. Dr. Grossman, too, had taken a special interest in my case. He asked all about the court appearance, and examined my wrists again to make sure they were healing properly.

Wednesday was finally behind me. I had survived the dreaded appearance in court and the anger of the district attorney. Little did I know that I would visit that courtroom many, many more times over the next year. Right now I was glad that this visit was over, and that God had been with me.

Early Thursday morning, I went over to the New York Fellowship offices for the Bible study B.J. had invited me to. I felt nervous because I figured I'd have to tell something about what had happened to me. I hadn't done that before in any kind of formal way, especially to a group of strangers.

The group was all male, mostly stockbrokers and bankers who work in the Wall Street area. B.J. led the discussion, which began with a passage of Scripture. Once the Bible study part of the meeting had concluded, B.J. turned to me and said, "Tom, why don't you share with the guys why you're here."

I guess that was my cue. Funny how my three years of seminary training and three years of pulpit ministry hadn't prepared me to speak from my heart, simply and straight-forwardly, about what God had done in my life. I felt intimidated by these men, and didn't know how they'd respond to my story. My initial reading was that they were sort of "macho" types, with a strong sense of camaraderie. They probably didn't know anyone who was gay, much less someone who had AIDS.

I took a deep breath and started. I managed to get out the accounts of the accident and my suicide attempt, but I couldn't bring myself to admit that I had lived a homosexual lifestyle and contracted AIDS. Afterward, I talked to B.J. in his office and said, "I wasn't as honest as I could have been, was I?"

"Don't worry, brother, there'll be time," he replied, putting his hand on my shoulder. "There'll be time. It was a beautiful testimony." Before I left, B.J. and I rejoiced together over yesterday's positive results in court.

There was still the matter of my job, however. A day or two later the personnel director at my office called back. My boss was willing to meet with me. *Finally I can go back to work*, I thought. When I walked into the building, I didn't see anyone I worked with except my boss's secretary; she greeted me warmly and held out her hand to me.

Then I went into my boss's office. He and the personnel director were standing there waiting for me.

They handed me a letter, which stated that I was resigning my position for personal reasons, and asked me to sign it.

I was aghast. I couldn't afford to lose this job; I needed the income to meet a number of significant financial obligations, and I especially needed my medical insurance coverage now that I had AIDS. Without my job I'd be ruined. I refused to sign the letter, and suggested several alternatives. The boss finally agreed to keep me on the payroll. I would continue at my current salary level for two more months, until May 1. Then I would be demoted to the same level as the people I had previously supervised, my salary would drop by twenty thousand dollars, and I would lose all supervisory responsibilities. "In fact," my boss said, "that [loss of supervisory authority] becomes effective immediately."

I didn't know what to say. I felt pinned against the wall and desperate enough that I'd do almost anything to keep from losing my job.

My boss continued, referring to the fact that I had AIDS. "You can stay in your office—I don't have any problem with that," he said, "but because there is so much fear among the other employees, I don't want to cause panic." He then proceeded to inform me that a separate bathroom would be assigned to me, and that an Out of Order sign would be posted on the door. A water fountain would also be similarly marked and designated for my use.

I emerged from that meeting, feeling shaken and betrayed by my employer. I was going through so much at that point that I mostly felt thankful that I still had my job. I would discover later, however, that my feelings would change.

For the next two weeks I continued to stay at Tony's. I still wasn't ready to return to my Connecticut apartment. It seemed that my entire life was in a state of limbo: As a new Christian, I felt as though I was learning to walk all over again. My job status remained uncertain and my legal case showed no signs of progress. I could sense this in Lee's voice when I called him (nearly every day) to see if the assistant DA had been willing to talk about a plea bargain. Lee told me that his repeated calls were never returned. This news discouraged me, but I didn't give up hope.

My second court date finally arrived, with about the same outcome as the first. Not only was Olivia's mother there again, but the assistant DA reported that the family had not changed its position on any of the charges and wanted to go ahead with a trial.

Judge Roberts again refused to accept this, and issued a strong warning: "I'm giving you one more chance to work out a deal. This is the last time you can appear in my court. You have two more weeks." He implied that if the assistant DA and the family would not attempt to work out a plea bargain, he might dismiss the entire case himself. The judge seemed to mean what he said; I only wished that his words would influence the assistant DA and the family.

Once this second court date had passed, I decided it was time to pull the pieces of my life together again. That meant returning to my apartment in Westport. When I arrived, my key wouldn't work in the door; the landlord had changed the locks. So I called and asked him to let me in. He came right over, let me in, and gave me a new key. He was incredibly friendly and supportive, just as Jerry had reported.

"Tom, don't let them get you down," he said to me. "You hang in there, buddy. We'll work with you on the rent—don't worry. We'll help you get things worked out."

I thanked him and went inside. I felt as if I had walked back in time to another world—to my old, hopeless, depressing world. The place was a wreck. During the three weeks before I attempted suicide I hadn't made my bed, done laundry, washed a single dish, or even scraped the food off. A foul smell came from the kitchen. Clothes were strewn everywhere. When I had packed my suitcase for my "final" plane trip, I had pulled out all kinds of outfits that I ended up leaving behind.

As I stood there looking at the mess, I realized that something had changed. *I* had changed. I had entered a new world, a new kingdom—the kingdom of God. I didn't want my old world any more. So I got to work cleaning up that apartment, feeling as though I was symbolically cleaning up my own life. What had happened to me with Peggy in Cedar Rapids was real, and my new outlook was now spreading to the environment I lived in.

Next to my bed I saw the suicide note I had left for Andrew. I crumpled it up and tossed it into the garbage. I no longer wanted to die. What I wanted now was to live, that is, to *really* live.

Into the midst of my despair and utter hopelessness came a shaft of light. The light was borne on the outstretched arms and in the warm voices of people who loved me—my sister and brother, my daughter, my parents, my friends, even people I didn't know who have since become some of my closest friends.

Receiving so much love rekindled an ability to love. My heart, which had been so stubbornly self-reliant, was softened and I began to experience life with a passion I hadn't known before. And through it all, I began to see God.

From a sermon Tom gave in early 1988

EIGHT
EIGHT
EIGHT
EIGHT
EIGHT

Amid all the uncertainty and confusion I was experiencing with the criminal lawsuit, the personal injury lawsuit, and my employer, I began to grow in my Christian life. I had so much to learn, and unlearn, about God and the Bible and the church. My seminary training twenty years ago had given me all kinds of information about theology and church history and the text of the Bible, but somehow it had clouded the fact that God was a real, living person who could indwell me and transform my life. Now I wanted to get to know that person better. I went to church at St. George's Episcopal, where Lee Ahlers had first taken me. Often I'd see B.J. and his family there. I joined the Sunday morning Bible study, and began to meet my own circle of friends. Gradually I started to feel like part of a Christian community.

When I embarked on this spiritual journey, I didn't realize that it would also be a journey of emotional healing. My conversion experience somehow unleashed a lot of pent-up emotion, like a wellspring inside me that sometimes bubbled up into tears, sometimes into laughter. Often the simplest thought or encounter would move me to tears—time alone with God, reflecting on my past, brief conversations with my family or others who cared about me. There were other times when I laughed harder than I could ever remember laughing before—deep, satisfying belly laughs.

During this period of time, three men in particular served as my spiritual and emotional mentors: a former Communist, a former pro football player, and a former monk. From them I learned not only how to seek, love and serve God, but I also experienced healthy, non-erotic male love and affection for the first time in my life.

My journey got off to a rocky start, however. A friend of B.J. suggested that I visit a group that ministers to people who want to get free from their homosexual orientation. The leaders, a husband-wife team, were charismatic Christians, and they believed that homosexuality was demonic. Their objective was to drive out the demons that cause a person to be homosexual.

I didn't know quite what to make of the group. It had an interesting mix of people: a few street hustlers, some businessmen, a few lesbians, and gay men. They got together on Friday nights to share and pray and lay hands on each other in order to exorcise the demons. They also spoke in tongues—a practice I had heard of, but never witnessed before. B.J.'s friend told me that others he'd sent to the group had been helped a great deal, so I figured I'd stick with it for a while.

Unfortunately, every week when the meeting ended, I would say to myself, *There's something wrong here, and I don't know what it is, but I don't think this approach is going to work for me.* Some of the people seemed a little extreme, and the speaking in tongues made me feel uncomfortable. And while I now believed that my former homosexual lifestyle was sinful, I couldn't buy the idea that I was demon-possessed.

I didn't want to go back. But since B.J.'s friend had recommended the group, I assumed that B.J. would approve of it, too. I kept thinking, *Maybe it's just me. I'm new to all this, so maybe I should just keep going.*

Finally I got up enough courage to confess my misgivings to B.J. "I just don't think this group is for me, B.J.," I said. "I'm having too much trouble with their theology or something."

B.J. sat back in his chair and said, "Well, I can understand that."

"What do you mean?"

He went on to explain that there were all different kinds of Christians who, while agreeing on the basic evangelical doctrines, differed widely when it came to specific interpretations of the Bible, styles of worship, and other issues. If I didn't feel comfortable in this group, he said, that would be fine. He didn't feel comfortable with everything they did, either. What's most important, he told me, was that I was seeking out other Christians for support and spiritual growth and that I should continue to look for a fellowship that fits me.

B.J.'s answer relieved me greatly. At least nothing was wrong with me for feeling weird at those meetings. I decided immediately to stop going, and asked B.J. if I could meet with him regularly instead.

Thus began the first and most significant of my three mentor relationships. B.J. started out as my spiritual counselor, but soon became my dearest and closest friend.

For the next few months I saw him two or three times each week. At first we talked a lot about homosexuality. B.J. gave me some helpful insights here. For example, at one point he said, "Let's not focus on *homo*sexuality; let's just talk about sexuality—what God's idea was when he created us as sexual beings. If you're sexually promiscuous, it doesn't matter whether you're homosexual or heterosexual as far as the Bible is concerned. It's whether you learn to express your sexuality as God intended: in the context of a loving, faithful marriage between a man and a woman. That's the only kind of intimate sexual behavior that is pleasing in God's sight. Anything else is sinful."

That made sense to me. It took the burden off of homosexual behavior, so that it wasn't any worse than other sexual sins such as adultery or premarital sex. As we talked, I realized he was not the fundamentalist I had at first supposed him to be. He didn't advocate the hellfire-and-damnation, homosexuals-are-an-abomination attitude. That made it easier for me to listen and learn.

B.J. did have some stereotypes about homosexuals, however. For one thing, he kept saying to me, "Tom, you don't look like a homosexual. You don't act like a homosexual." Before joining the Fellowship, B.J. had worked with the Lamb's Church in Manhattan for several years, talking to people in the streets about Christ. He had preached to male prostitutes, to transvestites, and to other overt types who flaunted their sexual perversion. So he assumed that all homosexuals were like these people.

"B.J.," I corrected him, "I couldn't begin to guess how many guys are walking the streets whom you would never suspect to be homosexual. They're all over, and they don't necessarily have limp wrists and speak in a feminine voice." I wasn't implying that he needed to be alarmed or afraid by this fact—I merely wanted him to know that homosexuals can be found in all different races, ethnic groups, and social strata, and that they don't all look and act alike. That was a new revelation to him.

He also thought it was impossible for two gay men to be friends without having sex. He thought the relationship was always sexual. At first, whenever I mentioned my friends, Tony, Andrew, and Will, I got the impression that he thought I should break off those friendships. I explained that these were genuine, meaningful friendships. "Those guys love me and I love them," I said. "It's not sexual. And besides, I've told them about my faith and my new stance on homosexuality—I don't have to stop being their friend. What better way is there to reach them than by loving them the way I was loved?" B.J. and I clashed over issues like this on occasion, but we were always able to talk it out. I'm sure I changed his thinking about many aspects of homosexuality; he also helped me gain a clearer understanding of the biblical view of sexuality.

We explored the Scriptures together often. He'd open his Bible, read a passage, and then say, "Well, what does this mean?" Together we would study it and discuss it. Again and again the truth of Scripture came through with the same freshness it had during my week at Peggy's.

But I still had an awful lot of questions. Just as I had been cynical of Peggy's simple answers, I half-expected B.J. to give me some of the same ones. I also carried many stereotyped notions of what a born-again Christian believed. So, rather than be timid, I asked B.J. straight questions when I didn't understand: "How can this be true?" "Why do you say that?" "Show me where the Bible says that." "That can't be what it means, can it?" B.J. fielded my questions thoughtfully and compassionately, and I slowly began to see that one really could be an intelligent person and believe that the Bible is true.

B.J. also talked a lot about grace and freedom. He helped me to strike a balance between the extremes of legalism and permissiveness. Grace is really freedom, he explained. Grace is not restriction. Christianity is not a set of rules and regulations: It's freedom. When we turn our lives over to Christ, he frees us to live the abundant life he created us for. Of course, the Bible also gives us guidelines to live by, but these guidelines enhance rather than limit our freedom.

My desire to grow spiritually spurred a renewed interest in reading. I hadn't looked at a single book about matters of faith in nearly twenty years; now I was developing a voracious appetite for spiritual reading. I began to set aside time each day to read (from the Bible and from other books), pray, and reflect. B.J. kept feeding me more books as fast as I could devour them. One that stood out was *Freedom for Obedience,* by Donald Bloesch, B.J.'s friend and former professor. Other books included *Mere Christianity* and other works by C. S. Lewis, *Celebration of Discipline,* by Richard Foster, and *New Seeds of Contemplation,* by Thomas Merton. I looked forward to these devotional times as opportunities to slow down and listen to the voice of God, to commune with him, to gain perspective on my life.

As B.J. and I shared our lives with each other, we discovered that our backgrounds were similar in many ways. Both of our fathers were pretty much uninvolved in our early lives. They had worked hard to provide for us, and they loved us, but somehow they didn't know how to communicate that love by spending much time with us, by befriending us. We concluded that our fathers had come from a generation of men who found it difficult to care for their sons at the emotional level. They had acted as head of the household, sole breadwinner, and so on, but they couldn't share their inner feelings or give us as much fatherly affection as we needed.

Many other factors came into play, but the result was that we both entered adult life with a skewed view of intimate relationships. B.J. drifted into heterosexual pro-miscuity and joined the Communist party. I drifted into homosexual promiscuity and pursued the gay lifestyle. B.J. had found God at age twenty-six in a Dubuque, Iowa, monastery. I had left God at age twenty-six, only to find him again at forty-six.

We talked about the importance of forgiving our fathers and not blaming them for our emotional troubles. They couldn't help it; they had done the best they knew how. Healthy fathering hadn't been modeled for them, either. So B.J. and I made a point of regularly praying for our fathers, along with our other needs.

And believe me, there were plenty of other needs. For one thing, I still struggled with occasional homosexual urges. They weren't so extreme that I was tempted to change my mind about Christ and return to the gay lifestyle, but they did tug at me sometimes when I'd pass a gay magazine rack or walk through Greenwich Village, where most of the gay bars are. I'd tell B.J. I was still feeling tempted, and he assured me that was normal. After all, I'd been in the gay lifestyle for twenty years; I couldn't instantly shut off all desire even though I knew lust is sinful. So I'd pray with B.J. for the strength to resist temptation.

Thankfully, alcohol did not particularly tempt me after my conversion. I knew how difficult it could be for some people to stop drinking after becoming addicted, and I greatly respected the help that Alcoholics Anonymous and its related groups have provided to so many. But I hadn't really gotten into a pattern of heavy, daily drinking until the three months leading up to my accident. Like so many problem drinkers, I drank to fill that empty place in me, the part of me that felt so alone and unloved. But when I rediscovered the love of my family and the love of God, my need to drink diminished considerably.

B.J. and I also prayed about my criminal lawsuit, which continued to drag on with no resolution. To my distress Burton Roberts ended up allowing my case to be assigned to a judge, which reduced the chances of a plea bargain or an early dismissal. I still feared that if the case went to trial, I'd have no defense and land in jail. Over and over I had to trust God to take care of me.

And my job situation had worsened, causing more tension. Word had spread around the office that I had AIDS. While some of my coworkers showed acceptance and support, others who used to be my friends began to completely avoid me. Some wouldn't shake my hand or touch me. Having to use a separate bathroom and water fountain only added to my humiliation at being demoted. With all my supervisory duties stripped away, I had very little to do at work. I began to get very angry at the way I was being treated because of my disease. So B.J. and I would pray for God's support and guidance in what to do about my job.

I would never have survived that period without these prayer times with B.J. They had a profound affect on me. To feel the love and support of a godly man, and to spend time alone with God filled a large vacuum in my soul. The feelings were enhanced, I'm sure, by B.J.'s unusual prayer routine—a carryover from his days in the monastery. In his office he had converted a small, four-by-five-foot closet into a prayer booth, completely bare except for a little chair, a few small icons, and a cross on the wall. We would squeeze into this little prayer closet, sit on the floor, and there in the darkness we would thank Christ for his light. Somehow that closet created an atmosphere where we could express ourselves freely to God and to each other. With only a sliver of light creeping under the door, we would pray and cry and laugh and sing hymns together, sometimes for as long as an hour. (Many of the old Methodist hymns I'd tried to forget over the past twenty years sprang back into memory.) And through it all, my spirit was being strengthened.

During those first few months with B.J., he played the role of pastor, teacher, and discipler to me. But as our friendship grew, I sensed that he wanted me to be less his student-counselee and more his partner in ministry. We spent more and more time together, and he asked me to join him when he traveled to retreats and speaking engagements. For that period of time, I basically turned my life over to B.J. It was all so exciting—never knowing from one week to the next where I'd be going or whom I'd be meeting. B.J. introduced me to many people, most of whom supported the Fellowship in some way. I met U.S. senators, Senate Chaplain Richard Halverson, professional athletes, CEOs of major corporations, and many other caring people from churches around the country. All the traveling and meeting people, I realized, was B.J.'s way of teaching me about relationships and intimacy.

Often he would ask me to tell my story to a church or a retreat group. People would come up to me afterward and tell me about close friends or family members who had AIDS or who were homosexual. They wanted to give hope to these people they loved, and apparently my words had brought encouragement.

During these times an awareness gradually sank in that this man B.J. really loved me. It was pure and genuine; he didn't want anything in return. For the first time in my life I found myself in a close relationship with a man who didn't ignore me or ridicule me on the one hand, or want sex with me on the other. He just accepted me and loved me.

Other people in the Fellowship noticed something special about our friendship, too. To them I was obviously more than one of B.J.'s "ordinary" counselees. They would say to me, "Do you realize how much B.J. loves you?"

One place B.J. took me was to the Trappist monastery in Dubuque, where he had become a Christian and spent several years of his life. On this same trip, I would meet the other two men who were to play a major role in my emotional and spiritual growth.

On the way there, B.J. and I stopped off in Chicago, where an anti-pornography demonstration was taking place. It also happened to be B.J.'s birthday. Several of his friends and supporters from the Citizens for Decency movement met us, and we all took B.J. out for a birthday dinner at Bennigan's.

Leo Wisniewski was one of these friends. A former noseguard for the Baltimore Colts, his six-foot-two, two-hundred-sixty-eight pound hulk immediately commanded one's attention. But inside that massive body was a gentle soul that truly loved the Lord. He had played pro football for eight years, and then decided he wanted to serve God in some kind of Christian ministry instead. So he set up a ministry to athletes at Penn State University, and he and his wife settled there. He had already heard about me from B.J., so when I was introduced to him, he greeted me with a big, warm hug. At dinner we all laughed and joked and horsed around, sometimes putting our arms around each other's shoulders.

At this point I still felt keenly aware of being touched by other men. What made this occasion—and any encounter with B.J. or his friends—so different was that these guys were expressing genuine, man-to-man warmth and affection without any of the sexual overtones I had gotten used to while in the gay lifestyle.

As these thoughts occurred to me, a funny thing happened. A group of women sat at the table next to us, and I accidentally overheard one of them who had been watching us say, "Look at those faggots." I suppose I could have been offended, but instead the remark tickled me. *If she only knew,* I thought, *I am the only one at this table with a gay background, but we are actually showing more genuine love than many homosexuals ever experience.*

The next day, B.J., Leo and I traveled on to the monastery. I had no idea what to expect, since I'd never been to one before. When we pulled up in our rental car, I saw that it was an old, old stone structure with an enclosed center section where the monks ate and slept. The rules forbade visitors from entering the monks' living quarters, but provided simple guest facilities on the second and third floors for people who wanted to have their own personal retreat.

Between twenty and thirty priest-monks live there. They are Trappists, a small monastic order that is dying out in this country. The contemplative Thomas Merton was perhaps one of the best-known Trappists. Originally, the monks in this order were not allowed to speak; they could only communicate in sign language. Now speaking is permitted.

We were shown to our guest rooms. Mine was tiny— much smaller than the smallest hotel room—and barren except for a single bed, a small writing desk, and a closet-sized bathroom to one side. A small crucifix hung on the wall over the bed.

Leo, who had visited before, offered to show me the chapel, the only new addition to the monastery. It had austere stone walls, simple pews, and a window in back that allowed a view of the trees. In front stood a plain altar, and behind it hung a modern, Giacometti-style sculpture of Christ on the cross.

I was somewhat overcome by this environment—its stark beauty and quietness. It felt like a holy place. I knelt there in awed silence, overwhelmed by a sense of God's presence. Leo knelt right next to me and comforted me by putting his arm on my shoulder. We sat there for about thirty minutes, until B.J. found us.

We went first to visit Father Matthias, the monk whom God used in B.J.'s conversion. He has since retired from the community and lives in his own little house just down the road from the monastery. He still runs shopping errands for the abbey and the monastery.

Father Matthias told me about his first encounter with B.J. many years before. At that time, B.J. had belonged to a radical Marxist group, and was visiting his parents in Dubuque. One day he had gone over to the monastery to buy bread for his mother. (The monks made and sold delicious bread.) Father Matthias had noticed this young man with hair down to his shoulders and a red headband, and had stopped him.

"You look interesting—what are you all about?" Father Matthias had said. Immediately B.J. had launched into a tirade against the church and against capitalism. The monk had listened and then said, "Hmm, that's interesting. Now let me tell you about myself." Something he had said had gotten through to B.J.; shortly thereafter B.J. turned his life over to God.

After we heard this story, B.J. said, "Okay, Tom, you and I have to go. Leo is going to stay here and have dinner with Father Matthias." He took me down the road to the abbey, where the nuns live. It is called Our Lady of the Mississippi Abbey because it overlooks the Mississippi River, and we arrived just in time for the six o'clock service. As we sat down in a small visitors' chapel off to the side of the main sanctuary, I heard singing—exquisite singing. But I couldn't see anyone. The sanctuary and chapel were empty except for us. The nuns, I found out, sat in long, narrow balconies along each side of the church, facing each other and singing their responses to the liturgy.

Their voices, crisp and clear as birds and utterly beautiful, filled the chapel. And the silences in between were deep and holy. About fifteen minutes later the singing stopped, and I could hear the nuns filing out to end the service.

Again overcome with emotion, I put my head down on the pew and wept. B.J. said nothing; he just let me cry. He had been overwhelmed by the Spirit of God in that place years ago. Now he was watching me experience the same thing.

B.J. and I ate dinner with the Mother Superior in a separate visitors' dining room. It was a simple meal—a bowl of barley soup, homemade cheese, and, of course, that wonderful homemade bread. Then the Mother Superior gave us a tour of the abbey. I saw where the other nuns ate in silence while one person sat on a little platform and read Scripture into a little microphone. The nuns wore plain white habits with black aprons over them. I saw the vegetable gardens and apple groves and a small candy factory where the nuns worked for four hours each day. (The rest of their time was spent in prayer and meditation.)

We ended up in a big library, where the nuns had gathered for "free time," an open discussion period held every evening. Father Matthias and Leo had arrived by this time, and I was asked to give my testimony to the group. As I spoke, I could tell the sisters were very moved by my story—so moved, in fact, that afterward they lined up and hugged me, one by one, as they went out of the room. Leo, who was hearing my story in person for the first time, stood at the end of the line. He embraced me with his enormous arms, lifting me off my feet. "Brother, that is so powerful," he said. "That really is a powerful story."

On the way back to the monastery, B.J. said that Father William might have arrived by now. He was coming up from Bolivia to report on several orphanages he oversees that the Fellowship supports. I had heard so much about Father William. Everyone at the Fellowship had said, "When you meet Father William, you'll want to take a pad of paper and follow him around so you can write down his wisdom." I had an image of him as an imposing, unapproachable, pious type who strutted around uttering profundities.

We parked the car and got out; it was nearly dark. As we approached the monastery, a door opened and a little, white-haired priest in a monk's habit came sprinting toward us. Hurriedly he hugged B.J. and gasped, "B.J., I've gotta talk to you, I've gotta talk." *Who is this guy?* I wondered.

"Okay, okay, just a minute," B.J. said. "I want you to meet my friend I've told you about. Tom Stribling, this is Father William." I was taken aback: I had expected to meet a quiet, peaceful priest who walked slowly with his eyes turned heavenward—not this hyperactive little ball of energy. I quickly recovered and said, "I've been looking forward to this moment."

"Thank you, thank you," he blurted, without looking me in the eye. He seemed preoccupied with whatever he wanted to tell B.J. about.

He quickly ushered us inside and down to a lounge in the basement. He was so wound up that he could hardly wait to tell B.J. about the orphanage situation. A year ago he had stumbled onto two government-operated orphanages with extremely substandard conditions. They were incredibly dirty and had no bathrooms or showers; a hole in the floor served as their toilet. Some of the children were infants who had been picked up from garbage heaps after their mothers had abandoned them.

Father William had met with officials of the Bolivian government numerous times, begging them to release legal responsibility for these orphanages to the New York Fellowship, who would install sanitary facilities and cover operating expenses. Just when he thought the government would give up control, on several occasions they backed out at the last moment.

Only a few weeks ago he had met with the First Lady of Bolivia, expecting her to sign over the orphanages, but again was told it couldn't yet be done. The whole experience had left him very frustrated over the plight of those dirty, helpless babies. He complained about all the political scheming going on there, and went over every detail of his endeavors.

It was all quite fascinating to me, but I had had a long, emotional day and felt tired. I announced that I was going to bed and excused myself. Barely distracted, Father William said, "Okay, Tom, you go to bed. Go to bed." I knew he had several more hours of talking with B.J. to do.

That was my first impression of Father William. I spent very little time with him the next day because he was so busy catching up with people. That evening I told my story to the monks, just as I had to the nuns, and the following morning we prepared to leave. Leo planned to take the car, because he had to conduct some local business, and B.J., Father William, and I were to get a ride to the airport for our return to New York.

Before Leo left, we walked down to the end of the driveway where the monks sold apples. We selected our own from several great bins and filled up a bushel basket, which Leo would later deliver to some nearby friends of B.J. When we had put the basket in his car, Leo told me how much he had enjoyed the time with me, and encouraged me to keep growing in my faith. Then he embraced me good-bye, and kissed me on the neck, a gesture that overwhelmed me.

As he drove away, he looked back and smiled, and for the second time in my life I realized that a man really loved and cared about me. To be affirmed by this big football player gave me a wonderful, warm feeling. In all my years of pursuing homosexual relationships, I had never felt such deep, pure love from another man. I walked back to the monastery with a big smile on my face, knowing I had made an important new friend.

At the airport Father William continued to defy my stereotyped images of a monk. I discovered he was a practical joker. When we stepped up to the ticket agent to check our bags, he pretended he had lost his tickets and proceeded to "search" all around for them. Then he looked down—there were his tickets on the floor. "Ah, here they are," he said, picking them up and handing them to the agent. Then he flashed a little mischievous grin to let me know he had dropped them on purpose.

When we changed planes in Chicago, B.J. pulled a prank on Father William. He had found somebody's name tag and stuck it on Father William's back. Father William traipsed around the terminal for some time before a man tapped him on the shoulder and said, "Excuse me, Father, but you have something on your back." When Father William saw the tag, he chuckled and said, "Oh, that B.J."

Father William asked me to sit next to him on the plane. Rather than ask me a lot of questions, he told me about himself. He had grown up as a street kid in Philadelphia, and his parents were both alcoholics. But they did go to the local Catholic church, where a priest there first presented the idea of joining a Trappist monastery. Something about the idea appealed to him, and at age nineteen he decided to go for it.

For the next sixteen years he led a life of prayer and meditation in Dubuque. Most of that time he lived by himself in a little hut—his "hermitage"—in the woods near the monastery.

"Tom," he said, "I would get up early, go into my little prayer closet and I would kneel on a hardwood bench and pray for fifteen hours. I did that every day for ten or eleven years. And you know what? At the end of all those years, I didn't know God any better than I had known him before."

His statement astonished me. I figured he'd say that all those years alone drew him *closer* to God.

"Well, how does a person get to know God, then?" I asked.

He didn't answer right away. He closed his eyes for a moment and stroked his marvelous beard, white as his thick head of hair.

Then he simply said, "Desire. Desire, my friend."

I began to understand what the others at the Fellowship meant about Father William. There was something very deep and wise about him. I wanted to soak up every word he said, and even though he didn't ask me much about myself, I felt as though he knew me—I felt connected to him somehow.

He went on to describe how he met B.J. Father Matthias, the chief human instrument in B.J.'s conversion, had introduced them. Father William and B.J. had hit it off immediately, and without seeking permission from his superior, Father William had asked B.J. to live in the hermitage with him. So each day B.J. had studied the Scriptures with Father William, and had slept on the floor at night.

All day they read Scripture and Father William explained it to B.J. They had also spent hours talking and listening to God in Father William's prayer closet. Several months later B.J. had moved down the road near the Abbey, where the nuns had fed him and given him a place to sleep. B.J. remained there four or five years, and continued to study with Father William. Eventually B.J. had moved on to seminary and the ministry, and Father William went to Bolivia to work with the orphanages.

As I listened to Father William on that plane, something came together in my mind. I started to see myself as a part of the "spiritual history" of Father William and B.J. Father William had taken in B.J. as a young Christian. And now B.J. was taking me in and helping me grow as a disciple of Jesus. This sense of having a spiritual heritage came over me; two generations of Christians had preceded me, and now I was the third. *Would I be the last generation*, I wondered, *or would there be more after me?*

Father William stayed in the country for several months after our first meeting. He mostly traveled and spoke to raise money for the orphanages, and periodically stopped into New York. Usually he'd stay with B.J., his wife Sheila, and their two children. I'd join them for dinner. I never had any prolonged time with him, but during his short visits he seemed to feed my spirit in a profound way. We also wrote long letters to each other.

B.J., Leo, and Father William. The love, the affection, the support, the spiritual counsel, the wisdom they shared had a transforming effect on my life. I felt myself changing, growing, deepening. My self-image and self-acceptance gradually improved. And even though I was encountering a great deal of stress, I felt happier than I had ever felt before.

I noticed change in another significant area of my life, too: my homosexual orientation. By now I'd heard stories about homosexuals who said they lost all homosexual desire the instant they gave their lives to Christ. Some, I'd heard, even claimed to have been changed from a homosexual to a heterosexual orientation. Neither of these was true for me. In the early months after my conversion, I still felt tempted and had to ask the Holy Spirit for strength to resist. I took practical steps such as avoiding the gay areas of town, talking regularly with B.J., and developing "straight" friendships and support networks.

As B.J. counseled me, he tended to downplay the homosexual issue. Rather than tell me I needed to change my orientation, he talked about growing in my relationship to Jesus who would fill me and empower me to live a full life that pleased Him. So I tried to focus on Jesus and avoid being obsessive about temptation.

Along with this counsel, of course, I was receiving something even more important: the consistent, pure, unconditional love from my friends and family, and especially from B.J., Leo, and Father William. I was getting more than spiritual platitudes—I was experiencing the truth in these people's lives. The shallow, fleeting thrills of my former lifestyle were being replaced with infinitely more satisfying Christian male love and affection.

The results began to show gradually, almost catching me by surprise. It occurred to me one day that I hadn't been tempted in a while. And as the months went by, when temptations did arise, I somehow found it a little easier to say no.

One night in particular, I went so far as to take a walk down into the Village, near some of my old haunts. I had been feeling lonely. In the past, whenever loneliness struck, I'd run straight for the gay bars and hang out. Now, as I strolled down the narrow streets, passing the quaint brownstones, streetlights filtering through the trees, something felt different. I heard the loud, driving dance music pulsating through the doors of the clubs. I watched as gay men in tight-fitting clothes floated in and out, their eyes moving up and down each other's bodies. I saw the familiar neon signs and glitzy marquees of places I'd frequented hundreds of times.

I looked at all of this, the world I had lived in for twenty years. What had that world given me? Little more than a string of empty relationships, twisted sex, and the disease that I would soon die from. I looked at all of this and I turned away. I didn't want any part of it any more. *Yes, God must be at work in my life*, I thought, and flagged a cab to take me home.

You have a right, perhaps even a sacred duty, to go through terrible confusion, searing doubt, horrible fear, and blasphemous anger toward a God whose ways are so far beyond the reach of our minds . . . who allows us to suffer tragedy upon tragedy, sorrow on sorrow. . . . How can we not cry out with tears: My God, don't you care?

That is what Jesus shouted out to God his Father from the cross. It is okay, now, for us to do the same. With Jesus, we will learn what it is to surrender to a Love we cannot understand. With his cry, ours will be heard. . . .

It is not less Love, because we cannot understand it. It is not less our Eternal Life, just because it puts us to death in the flesh. He is not less lovable, just because his goodness prunes and purifies and baptizes us in fire until we cannot, in our mortal selfishness, endure the pain any longer. Even if he kills us, Tom, and he will, we will believe in him, in his Love which he has made us know and which he is preparing us to receive in all its fullness forever.

From a letter Father William sent Tom, July 1988

NINE
NINE
NINE
NINE
NINE

I had a lot to face after I became a Christian—specifically, how much my past life had hurt other people and myself. There were so many harmful actions and decisions that I now had to take responsibility for. I had abandoned my daughter and my wife. I had created all kinds of pain and embarrassment for my parents and my siblings. I had probably passed on the AIDS virus to a number of guys before I began taking precautions. And then there was the accident, the emotional trauma, and irrevocable physical damage I had inflicted upon Olivia. I found myself experiencing frequent bouts with grief and remorse over all I'd done. Sometimes the briefest reflection on my past— often when I was alone—would trigger a rush of tears. I'd ask myself, *If Christianity is such a big deal and is supposed to make me joyful, then why am I crying all the time?*

Father William helped me deal with that question even before I asked him. On one of his visits to New York, he led a morning Bible study I'd been attending at the Fellowship. We were studying the Beatitudes, and when we read the verse, "Blessed are those who mourn, for they will be comforted" (Matthew 5:4), he brought up a subject I'd never heard of: "holy grief." He said that one kind of mourning Christians feel is a sense of sorrow over their past sins.

Something struck me about this idea. I said to the group, "I know that I'm still grieving, but why? I thought Christians were forgiven their sins. So why am I crying all the time?"

Father William looked at me and said, "Tom, you're a prime example of what I'm talking about. Your life has been so full of grief and tragedy. But the grief you're feeling now is a holy grief—a grief that's been transformed. That's a good sign. You've been saved and redeemed, Tom, so you don't need to carry any guilt. But you've got to go through this period of holy grief. Unless your heart is broken, you cannot feel compassion and mercy."

Right away I understood. Yes, my sins were forgiven, but in order for me to put the guilt behind me, I had to accept responsibility for my sins and grieve over them. It was a difficult, emotional phase to go through. It took nearly six months for me to come out of this grieving period.

Of all the things I felt guilty about, I found that the accident and the injuries I had caused Olivia were the hardest for me to accept God's forgiveness for. I knew that God had forgiven me, but I couldn't fully accept that forgiveness. Every time I thought about the terrible suffering she was going through in the hospital—all on my account—guilt would overwhelm me once again. Because of me, her life would never be the same, and there was nothing I could do about it.

In April 1987, when my case had been assigned to a judge—all but guaranteeing that it would go to trial—I had left the courthouse completely deflated. We hadn't gotten our plea bargain. We had lost Judge Burton Roberts; there would be no further chances to appear before him. I had been told the new judge, Robert Seewald, had a reputation for being fair. But if there were no plea bargain, the case would go to trial, and since my charges carried a mandatory prison sentence, what could he do? I was definitely the one who had struck Olivia; there had been witnesses.

Lee Ahlers and I were given a month to prepare for our first appearance with Judge Seewald. By this time the assistant district attorney had softened somewhat, giving me a glimmer of hope. In court he and Lee approached the bench to talk with the judge "off the record," which means that the conversation does not appear in the official court report. Since I sat close to the front, I was able to hear what they were saying.

"Your Honor, we don't really want to prosecute this case," the assistant DA said. "However, in this situation we are dealing with an adamant, bitter family. It is a very strong policy of the New York City criminal court system to honor the wishes of the victims in personal injury cases. Because the family does not want to plea bargain, my hands are tied."

Judge Seewald said, "Well, then, let's postpone for three weeks. In the meantime see if you can reason with the family."

The family refused to bargain in any way. Several more postponements. The assistant DA still wouldn't return Lee's calls.

In June, Lee filed a "motion for dismissal in the interest of justice." He referred to statements from Dr. Grossman about my AIDS condition, and that the stress of my having to go through a trial, not to mention imprisonment, would cause my health to deteriorate even more rapidly. He quoted the psychiatrist I had seen who indicated that I had stabilized emotionally and was not likely to repeat my actions. He even mentioned that B.J. Weber had informed him of my commitment to Jesus Christ, and that I was "receiving tremendous strength in the forgiveness of Christ."

Lee continued to explain that I had no prior criminal record, and had faithfully served society as a minister and in the educational field, and therefore that I posed no danger to the community. He indicated that I had no intention of driving again. If I were sent to jail, he said, the public would have to bear the cost of my complex medical treatment (seventy-five to one hundred thousand dollars). And according to Dr. Grossman, I would most likely die in jail, since my life expectancy was only about a year. "No purpose would be served by prosecuting this matter further," he said in closing.

The assistant DA promptly replied with an "affirmation in opposition" to the dismissal motion, citing the "seriousness of the offense"; the great harm I had inflicted on Olivia, who was still in the hospital; the fact that I was clearly guilty; and several other factors. Lee's motion, he said, "does not provide compelling reasons to dismiss this indictment and should be denied."

Again, Judge Seewald put off making a decision.

My frustration and anxiety grew as the delays continued. Every three weeks it was the same thing: We went back into court, the assistant DA would tell the judge that the family's position hadn't changed, and the case would be postponed. Everyone acted as if they were caught in the middle: the assistant DA, the judge, Lee. To me, it felt as though every court appearance brought me one step closer to jail. To them, however, every delay (they hoped) would give the family more time to submit to a plea bargain. There seemed to be no end in sight.

Along the way I picked up bits of information about Olivia's condition. Her injury was very serious, and for some time the doctors worried that they might not be able to save her right leg. About sixteen times she had undergone reconstructive surgery, which included bone grafts, skin grafts, and nerve implants. The more I heard about all she was going through, the more I wanted to visit her at the hospital and tell her how terrible I felt about what had happened. I wanted her to hear it from me, not through a lawyer. But Lee advised me not to see her, because in his experience such an action could sometimes make matters worse for the family.

That summer Lee asked if he and B.J. could meet with me about an important matter. As we sat in B.J.'s office, Lee proceeded to tell me that he had accepted a position with the district attorney's office in the Bronx— the very district attorney who was prosecuting me. As a result, he could no longer represent me in my case. He assured me that he was completely behind me, and that he would not be involved in any way in prosecuting me.

His announcement caught me completely by surprise, but before I had a chance to worry about what to do now, Lee said, "I've already contacted a young man named Mark Gombiner, who is one of the most brilliant criminal lawyers I know of in the city. I've discussed your case with him, and he's willing to take it if you approve."

I felt nervous about having to change lawyers. But another part of me thought, *Maybe this new guy will be able to break through the stalemate somehow.*

I met with Mark in his Soho office. He was in his late twenties and rail-thin; the suits he wore made him look like a coat hanger. He had specialized in criminal law at Boston Law School, and he and his partner were devoting most of their efforts to criminal cases in which the defendants had been set up or were victims of society. I liked him. When he went over all the implications of my case, I liked him even more. It was obvious that he knew the law inside out. He had a straightforward, no-nonsense style. I felt relieved, and confident that Lee had passed me on to an extremely competent lawyer.

Still, the proceedings dragged on. Practically every-thing was said "off the record," because the assistant DA didn't want the record to show that he didn't want to prosecute. And Judge Seewald hadn't made his feelings clear, either on or off the record. Mark and I didn't know where he stood.

Virtually every time we were in court, Olivia's mother was present. She lived in Illinois, but had apparently made arrangements to stay in New York while Olivia was in the hospital—six and a half months altogether. Judge Seewald always treated her with respect, and always remained noncommittal about his position on the case. He regularly asked her if there was anything she wanted to say. Each time she refused. Though she appeared absolutely determined to put me behind bars, she also seemed afraid to speak in public.

Then one day, six or seven months into the case, she didn't show up. I didn't know the reason—she had a schedule conflict, perhaps, or had to return to Illinois. The assistant DA and Mark went before the bench again to speak off the record, as usual. Mark said, "Your Honor, let's just face the facts here. Look at Mr. Stribling. He's a well-educated man, a seminary graduate. He has never been in jail before, never even been arrested before. There's no question that he had a tragic and unfortunate accident. He is dying anyway. Mr. Stribling does not belong in jail."

For the very first time I heard the judge say where he stood. He simply said to Mark, "You are right, I know that." Upon hearing these words, I felt a tremendous sense of relief. The family's position hadn't changed, and the case was postponed again, but at least I had reason to hope.

Enduring so many court appearances with no resolution in sight was hard enough, but hearing about Olivia's condition distressed me greatly. She had gotten out of the hospital in time to return for the fall semester at her college in Illinois. From the information I was given, I heard she organized a Students Against Drunk Drivers chapter there. At first she was confined to a wheelchair; eventually, I was told, she learned to walk on her own, though not without a serious limp. Her right leg was deformed, as well as part of her back, where some bone and muscle tissue had been removed.

I wanted so badly to contact her somehow, tell her how upset and concerned I was about her. I asked Mark again if I could write her a letter, and he said he didn't think it would be wise. I sat down and wrote her several letters anyway, but stuck them in a drawer. One of them went like this:

Dear Olivia:

We have never met, and I am having a difficult time knowing how to start this letter. I just feel that I can't let any more time go by without trying to convey to you how deeply sorry I am for the pain you and your family are now feeling because of my negligence.

I have no recollection of the accident. I don't know how it happened or even what happened, but I do know, through third parties, that you are seriously hurt and are suffering a great deal. I pray for you daily that your body will be restored to its normal state and that you will, in time, overcome the trauma that the accident must have created for you.

I understand that this expression of my concern may be of little comfort to you right now. It's not my intention to change whatever feelings you may have about me. But I do want you to know how deeply sorry I am, and how strongly I wish for your complete recovery.

All of my expressions of concern, and my offers to do what little I can to help you (which I've only been able to convey through lawyers) are genuine. And even though that is the case, I can understand your reluctance to accept them. I have a daughter who is only one year younger than you, and I know how I would feel if the same thing had happened to her.

Please know that this letter is not meant to influence you, but rather to let you know that I am not oblivious to the pain you are suffering.

I have had to reexamine my own life and have experienced the pain of soul-searching that comes with the awareness that my actions have caused injury and pain for someone else.

Regardless how the courts may decide my fate, I will continue to deeply regret what has happened, and earnestly pray that you will be able to resume your life in every way as you were living it before the accident.

Sincerely,
Tom Stribling

As I wrote these letters, I sometimes struggled with serious doubts about the goodness of God. *How could you allow Olivia to go through all this suffering?* I'd say to God. *She did nothing to deserve it. At least I can say I brought my problems on myself. But what about her? What can she say?*

The more I wrestled with these questions, however, and talked with B.J. and Father William about them, I realized that there was no answer to them. There was nothing I could say. God is too big and too beyond comprehension for me or any other human being to understand. I could never know why such a tragic accident would happen to Olivia. Neither could I understand why my life would soon be cut short, even though I had just begun to live my life for God.

I didn't know why such things happen, but I refused to believe that God causes them. Instead, I concluded that God may possibly *use* a tragedy, in his own mysterious way, to bring about some kind of good in that person's life, or to somehow bring glory to himself. I didn't even try to guess how God might use Olivia's tragedy for good, but I prayed every day that he would.

Meanwhile, the legal stalemate continued into 1988.

Judge Seewald maintained his opinion (off the record) that even though I did not belong in jail, he would neither dismiss the case nor recommend probation for me as long as the family stuck by their original position. So he would stall every time. By now Olivia's mother had engaged a different lawyer because the high-powered firm she had first retained realized that I had no assets and therefore couldn't come through with a big settlement. Mark reported to me that their new lawyer was a friend of Olivia's family and a small-time operator compared to the previous firm.

Mark started calling this new lawyer and trying to talk him into convincing the family to negotiate. Each time the lawyer would respond, "Hey, I'm only doing what the family wants. There is a serious injury here. This poor girl is damaged for life. There is no chance of a plea bargain."

The standoff reached a point where Judge Seewald began to get impatient. He finally said, "Look, how long is this going to go on? I've given you guys how many postponements now, and you haven't been able to work anything out. I am going to give you one more chance to settle this thing. If you haven't worked anything out in three weeks, then we are going to go to trial."

His stern warning scared me. If nothing were worked out, then a jury would be selected for a trial. Witnesses would testify that they saw me strike Olivia with my car. If the jury pronounced me guilty to the charges I was facing, then the judge would have no choice but to send me to jail.

Sometime during those three weeks a miracle occurred.

Mark called me and said, "Tom, I think I've got some good news. I just received a call from another lawyer. The family has engaged another lawyer, and they are willing to talk."

I could hardly believe what I was hearing. Apparently Olivia's father, previously uninvolved in the proceedings, had stepped into the picture. He obtained a new lawyer, who then arranged to meet with Mark to discuss a settlement. Olivia's father even went to one of the meetings. Mark told me afterward that the father, who couldn't have been a nicer guy, made it very clear that he had no desire to put me in jail, but that the family did want some financial relief for all the medical expenses that had built up.

In a very short time we worked out a written agreement. The family would drop the most serious charge, first-degree assault, which carried a mandatory jail sentence. In return, I agreed to plead guilty to the remaining charges, name Olivia as the beneficiary of my fifty-thousand-dollar life insurance policy, and guaranteed that I would continue paying the premiums on that policy. I also agreed to cooperate with the family's lawyers in any other civil lawsuits they might bring against other parties. (The family wanted to go after the owner of the bar I visited on the night of the accident. Under Connecticut law, the owner can be held responsible for serving alcohol to an obviously drunk person who then causes an accident or injury. So I agreed to name the bar.)

I met Olivia's father and the new lawyer when we signed the agreement. (Her mother wasn't there.) The father was very cordial to me and asked about my health. Judge Seewald was pleased when we presented the settlement to him in court. We were to meet in two weeks for sentencing, and then it would be over.

For the last time in court I stood before Judge Seewald. Olivia's mother, grandmother, aunt, and uncle were present. The assistant district attorney said that "the people" have agreed to drop the charge of assault in the first degree.

The judge said to me, "How do you plead to the rest of the charges?"

"I have no recollection of the accident, Your Honor," I replied, as Mark had coached me.

"Well then, how do you know that you're guilty?" the judge said.

"Your Honor, when I was presented with the evidence against me, I realized that there was no other possibility."

"In other words," he said, "it was you in that car on that night?"

"Yes, that is correct. Based on the evidence that has been presented to me, I am confessing to my guilt and am remorseful."

The assistant DA then said, "Your Honor, the claimant's mother is in court, and she would like to read a statement into the record."

For the first time in all these proceedings, I heard Olivia's mother speak. She stood up and read from a three-page, typed statement in a manila folder. She said that drunk driving was criminal and that because of my drunk driving, her daughter's life had been irrevocably changed. Olivia was once beautiful and had hoped to be a dancer, but that would never happen now—because of me. She said that I had continued to live my life with apparently no concern for Olivia or her family—that I hadn't been denied anything because of my reckless actions. She felt it was criminal that I was not being put behind bars.

"The only thing that gives me any satisfaction," she concluded, "is knowing that God has already punished Mr. Stribling by giving him AIDS. I wonder how this case would have turned out if he didn't have AIDS." Then she sat down.

Her harsh words really upset me. I didn't look at her.

Fortunately, the judge gave me a chance to respond. I pulled myself together and said, "I would like the claimant and her family to know how sincerely I regret the injury that I caused their daughter, and the hardships my actions have caused for them. I wish I could take back the events of that evening, but of course I can't. I was advised by my attorneys not to communicate with Olivia or her family, but I want them to know that Olivia has been constantly in my thoughts and prayers. I hope at some point that they will be able to forgive me."

Judge Seewald then issued my sentence: Five years' probation, and two hundred hours of community service. (By this time I had begun ministering to people with AIDS, and he said I could continue that ministry as community service.) Further, I had to surrender my driver's license, name Olivia as the permanent beneficiary of my insurance policy, and agree to cooperate with the family in any other lawsuits.

It was over. As the judge cracked his gavel to adjourn the court, I felt a giant burden lift from my shoulders—but not the burden of Olivia's suffering, however. I would probably carry that burden to my grave. But at least I wouldn't have to face the prospect of dying in jail. I could still serve God with whatever time I had left to live.

A few weeks ago a new friend of mine, Robert, told me about his friend Paul who was hospitalized with pneumocystis carinii pneumonia. Just weeks before entering the hospital, Paul had prayed to receive Christ into his life. Robert asked me if I would go to the hospital to visit Paul.

When I entered Paul's room, I was immediately struck by his appearance. He was thin, and his skin was a very pale, almost translucent, white. With his light brown hair spread against his pillow and about five days' growth of beard on his face, he looked very much like an artist's concept of Jesus.

Unfortunately, Paul recovered from the pneumocystis only to succumb to a second infection. He died on Good Friday at the age of thirty-three. Robert told me that Paul's earnest prayer before he died was to be more like Jesus Christ.

Paul's prayer was answered. Not only was he like Christ in his death, but we have the assurance as Christians that he is now communing with Christ in an eternity that we can only long for.

From Tom's New York Fellowship AIDS Ministry newsletter, April 1988

TEN
TEN
TEN
TEN
TEN

After my conversion, I hadn't initially thought much about returning to the ministry. I felt I had so much to learn that I needed people to minister to me—people like B.J., Father William, and others. But as the months passed, I gained a growing sense that God wanted me to serve him in a special way with the time I had left.

Several developments, all of which were going on during the court proceedings, helped me to arrive at this conclusion. For starters, there had been the practical reality of my job and my financial situation. I had been slapped with a twenty-thousand-dollar pay cut, and had quickly realized that I couldn't meet my obligations to creditors. I was forced to file for bankruptcy, yet another humiliating process. I still had a job of sorts—as well as my absolutely essential health insurance coverage—but I also had been getting the message loud and clear that my employer was not eager for me to stay around.

I began to think about what kind of employment to pursue, and talked to B.J. about it. "Well, brother," he said, "maybe you should consider joining us here at the Fellowship. If you want to come here, we'll help support you."

His answer struck a chord. *Of course—that would be a natural for me*, I thought. I could renew my relationship with the Methodist church, and with B.J.'s and the

Fellowship's support, I could begin working with people who have AIDS. It would be a meaningful way to spend the however-many-months of my life that remained.

I didn't quit my job immediately; I stayed on for another six months. During this time I met and traveled with B.J. regularly to try to put together and raise support for an AIDS ministry. (My employer had told me I was free to take as much time off as I wanted—not so much out of generosity, I think, but because they felt too uncomfortable having me at the office. Nevertheless, I took advantage of the offer.)

A second development was that I noticed the way people responded to me when I told my story. B.J. took me around the country to speak to churches that support the Fellowship. Basically I described what God had done in my life, and urged them to consider how their church could meet the physical and spiritual needs of people with AIDS. After hearing me speak, several churches initiated their own ministry to AIDS patients, and several others offered to contribute money to my own efforts.

Even beyond this generally positive response, I began to notice that many people were moved at a personal level by my words. Often people would come up after I had spoken and share their own hurts with me, asking for my advice. I had trouble understanding this at first because I rarely felt I was playing the role of "teacher" or "counselor" or "imparter of wisdom." I simply wanted to tell others about how my life had been overrun by the love of Christ. But something about the way I told my story touched people—even people who weren't Christians. Perhaps it was that all the events in my life seemed so fresh to me, and my feelings—of pain and remorse, as well as peace and joy—were so close to the surface. But I also think people could sense that I had truly encountered God in a personal way, and that the changes he was bringing about in my life were real.

One of the first times I spoke publicly was to a group of ten lawyers in Dallas during their lunch hour. B.J. knew a couple of them and had arranged the informal meeting. He introduced me by saying, "This is Tom Stribling, and he has had a miraculous experience that he'd like to share with you."

I told the whole thing from beginning to end, with no holds barred. I hadn't yet been able to give my testimony without choking on my tears at various points. The entire time I spoke, their attention was riveted on me, and several of them were visibly moved.

When I had finished, one of the men, a junior executive in the firm, asked me into his office. He sat down and said, "Tom, do you think it is possible for a homosexual to change?" (I got the distinct feeling he was struggling himself.)

"Well, I don't really know the answer to that," I said. "I can't say that I've changed, but I do know that God has given me the strength to withstand the temptation." He thanked me, and I left.

As it turned out, only two of the ten men in the meeting were Christians—the two men B.J. knew. "Why didn't you tell me?" I protested afterward.

"Because you would have said things differently and omitted some things if you had known," B.J. replied with a grin.

On that same trip to Texas B.J. and I visited the Presbyterian Church in Houston, where I spoke to their large congregation and to a Sunday school class of two hundred. They, too, were captivated. In fact, shortly after our visit, the church began its own full-fledged ministry to people with AIDS. One couple from that church, Dan and Deenie Reese, took a special interest in me—but not immediately. They had known B.J. for a long time, and when he told them he was bringing a new friend with him to Houston, they were eager to meet me. Eager, that is, until

B.J. told them I had AIDS; then they hesitated. They agreed to take B.J. and me sailing, but preferred that I not stay with them on my first visit. It seemed they knew little about AIDS, and were simply afraid. But everything changed during that glorious afternoon of sailing on the Gulf. After hearing me describe what God had done in my life, they, too, were moved and wanted to help me pursue an AIDS ministry.

I sensed that people like Dan and Deenie were genuinely touched by my message: that God's love had broken into my life, filling me with peace and purpose, and that they could share this same love with others who suffered with AIDS.

Father William must have picked up on the change in me, too. After that weekend at the monastery when we first met, he had turned to me and said, "Tom, I don't say this to frighten you, but you may be a saint."

His remark had embarrassed me. Even though I had only spent a few hours with him, I had immediately felt as though he knew me. He didn't need to get into a prolonged discussion, or ask me to rehash my experiences or my childhood. He just knew that God had transformed me, and had felt it in my presence. So I had also felt strongly affirmed.

Later, Father William expanded on his comment to me in a letter: "God has given you a special call to be a witness, Tom, that is rare in the Christian community," he wrote. "Jesus came to you in an extraordinary way. You are a witness to that, before believers and unbelievers. And then, you are a man who is dealing with potentially imminent death. You are doing so as a Christian. You go on believing in and testifying to Love. That is impossible on merely human grounds. There must be 'something' more than human in your experience to account for your faith. We who receive your witness cannot miss the suggestion: That 'something' beyond the human known by

Tom—might it not be the very Love he is announcing to us in his faith?''

As B.J. and I spent more time working together, we agreed that I should move back into the city to be closer to the Fellowship offices, which at that time were in the Wall Street financial district. For a few weeks I lived in the office itself, which happened to have a sofa bed, shower, and kitchenette. Then a man who supports the Fellowship heard about an apartment in Battery Park City, located within six or seven blocks of the office, and graciously offered to pay half the rent if the Fellowship picked up the rest. So I moved into this apartment, and continued to lay the groundwork for an AIDS ministry.

To retain my ordination in the Methodist church, I had to meet with the ministerial credentials committee, explain my renewed commitment to Christ, talk about my disease, and answer their questions.

I wasn't prepared for their response. Half of the twelve-member committee were deeply moved by my story. The other half scratched their heads, not quite understanding what had happened to me. In the ensuing discussion, several of them freely stated that they were gay and found nothing wrong with it. They didn't seem to grasp why my position on homosexuality had changed. Perhaps they worried that in my zeal I would run around New York, bashing homosexuals with the Gospel and ascribing them all to hell. That, of course, was not my purpose at all. I wanted to bring the love of Christ to people with AIDS; what happened in their hearts after that was between them and God. I simply wanted to be available to talk or pray with them.

I left the meeting, feeling very distraught and doubtful that my ministerial credentials would be renewed. As it turned out, the committee finally did approve my reordination, though by a narrow vote. The bishop then gave me a special appointment to pursue this ministry.

With B.J.'s help, I put together a mailing list of my own friends and relatives, and supporters of the Fellowship who would be particularly interested in my work. Dan and Deenie Reese graciously offered to provide a major portion of my operating expenses. I sent out an occasional newsletter describing my ministry and asking for prayer and monetary support. All the while, we were meeting nearly every day to read Scripture and kneel before God in B.J.'s prayer closet.

Next, I began going around to hospitals and inquiring about the AIDS patients there. I found that it wasn't easy to get permission to do what I wanted to do. I couldn't just walk in the door and ask to talk to an AIDS patient. They would tell me I had to have the name of a specific person. Some hospitals didn't like the fact that I was a minister— they thought I'd try to force religion on their patients. Eventually, I arranged to visit two hospitals on a regular basis: the Veterans Administration Hospital at 23rd Street and 1st Avenue, and St. Vincent's Hospital, a Catholic facility on 11th Street in Greenwich Village.

The VA management allowed me to visit on a "volunteer" basis, and told me not to discuss religion unless someone requested it. That arrangement suited me fine. At St. Vincent's I could meet with patients as a clergyman. The chaplain there, who was very cooperative, would give me a computer printout of recently admitted AIDS patients, and I would go introduce myself.

I called on many people in these hospitals, as well as on patients in other hospitals who asked for me, were referred to me, or who answered the ad I had placed in the *PWA* [People With AIDS] *Coalition Newsline*. My approach was simple and informal. I let them know I wanted to be their friend. I held their hand, offered them comfort, and told them I also had AIDS.

My offer of friendship, I discovered, meant so much to them. Many had been disowned by their families, or else their families lived far away and were largely unavailable. These men had no one to talk to. Even their circle of friends in the gay community, which is normally close-knit, seemed to fall apart when someone got AIDS. (I believe it's too much of a reminder that they too are mortal and at high risk.)

It wasn't my style to club them over the head with the Gospel. (I remembered how angry and defensive I became when B.J. confronted me so directly. He now says he would have handled that situation differently.) So I didn't walk into someone's hospital room and say, "Do you know Jesus Christ? Do you realize your homosexuality is a sin?" Instead, I listened as they talked about their own hurts, worries, and fears. They are keenly aware of being perched on the edge of eternity, and many also feel remorseful about their past lifestyle; I didn't usually have to say much to get them talking about the ultimate issues of death and God and the afterlife. As they brought up these questions, or as a natural opportunity presented itself, I would share with them how Christ's love has made such a difference in my life. If I felt it was appropriate, or if they requested it, I would say a short prayer with them.

Several months after I began visiting hospitals, I received a call from a woman who had seen my ad. She was calling on behalf of her friend Roger, who was a vice president of a large New York department store. Roger was in the hospital with AIDS, and had asked her to come and pray with him during her lunch hours. He had also said that he wanted to see a minister.

As she talked, I felt serious misgivings about meeting Roger. I didn't think I'd like this guy. From what I knew of him, he was probably typical of the snobbish, East Side gay men of the kind I had never liked during all my years in the gay community. They were elegant, overindulgent dressers with an uppity, high-society air about them. In spite of my reluctance, I told the woman I'd visit Roger.

To my surprise, we hit it off immediately. Roger was nothing like the person I had expected him to be; we established instant rapport. He got right to the point. "There are two things that are bothering me," he said. "One is that I haven't told my parents that I'm gay or that I have AIDS. I've told them I'm in the hospital and that I have cancer, but they don't know I have AIDS or that I've been living with a male lover for the past twenty years."

I could identify with his fear. I had been in the same position. Somewhere along the line my parents had realized I was gay, but they knew nothing of the lifestyle I was living. And even after my suicide attempt, I had told Peggy, Jerry, and Paula—but not my parents—that I had AIDS. I explained to Roger that I had only recently gotten up the courage to tell my parents about my disease, and that it had meant a lot to both of us.

"I think your parents really want to know," I said.

Roger listened to me, and then continued. "The other thing that's bothering me is that I'm wondering whether or not God is displeased with the way I've chosen to live my life."

For some reason my initial impulse was to jump in and tell him that God does not approve of the homosexual lifestyle, and that God had told me it was wrong. As I started to say a few words to this effect, I saw him stiffen up and even inch away from me in his bed. It occurred to me that I was taking the wrong approach, so I caught myself.

Instead, I simply said, "Roger, I think that if you really want to know the answer to that question, God will reveal it to you. He'll let you know if he has been displeased."

That seemed to satisfy him.

A week or two later I got another call. Roger was in critical condition and semi-comatose. So I hurried back to the hospital, upset that maybe I had missed my opportunity to talk about Christ. Roger didn't know I was in the room, but his lover happened to be there. I prayed with both of them.

"Have his parents been contacted?" I asked his lover.

"Yes, he called them himself," he said. "They came to see him. In fact, they're in the city now. We told them Roger has AIDS."

Roger's condition improved. When I visited him again, he was sitting up in bed, looking much better.

"I understand you told your parents," I said.

"Yes, I did, Tom. You know, they love me even more than I thought they did. They were very loving and understanding."

"That's great, Roger."

"You know what else?" he said. "I believe God has revealed something to me. I don't want my lover to hear this, but I don't think God has been very pleased with my choice of homosexuality. I'd like for you to pray with me."

I bowed my head and began by mentioning the need for repentance. Roger picked right up on what I was saying, and prayed to God in his own words: "God, please forgive me of all my sins, including the way I have lived my life. I'm very sorry, and I hope that you'll forgive me. I want Christ to come into my heart."

It was an incredible moment—the very first conversion I had personally witnessed. Even though I hadn't really done much myself to lead him to Christ, I felt great. Roger had been ready; I had been there to help. As I reflected on my initial hesitation in seeing him, it hit me that I, who have experienced my share of prejudice by non-gays, carried some of my own prejudices about certain kinds of gay people. Meeting Roger served to remind me that anyone can be spiritually hungry and that the grace of God excludes no one.

Afterward, I ran back to the Fellowship and told B.J.,

and we rejoiced together. Roger lived for another couple of months, and I visited him regularly until he moved to a different hospital in New Jersey. Then I talked to him on the phone nearly every day until he died.

Another wonderful encounter was with Bill, the man whose actress friend Polly Holliday had called me about. I was so moved when he told me that his life was not complete, and that he wanted me to pray with him. And then to hear him groan with grief before Jesus, ask for forgiveness, and invite him into his heart—made me feel as though I was part of a holy miracle in this man's life. I saw him several more times after his confession. Polly sat with him the day before he met God face-to-face.

Of course, the number of conversions I witnessed was small compared to the number of people I visited. I longed for every person I spoke with to experience the liberating love of Christ—as I had. But I also felt that it was God's responsibility, not mine, to bring people to the point of asking him into their lives. So I viewed myself as more of a facilitator, a friend, a messenger of comfort to those I met. I was ready to talk about Christ when appropriate, and often did. But I also believed that every hand I touched, every word of encouragement, every prayer I uttered, brought glory to God—regardless of the person's response.

One man I spent considerable time with, Steve, did not to my knowledge become a Christian. But I felt God used me to bring about some healing in his life. He was a very angry man, and had cut himself off from everyone in his family except his sister, who happened to be a Christian. She called me from her home in Boston and told me about Steve. When I asked for his name and hospital so I could visit him, she hesitated, fearing that Steve would feel too intruded upon. Finally she consented.

Surprisingly, Steve said sure, he'd be glad to see me. He was warm and friendly, but made it clear that he did not want to discuss Jesus Christ. (He had gotten heavily involved in New Age philosophy.) So I didn't push the issue of faith. He asked if I'd come back again.

Shortly thereafter, his sister called again. Even though he had specifically told them not to, Steve's parents were coming to New York to see him. She and her husband would be coming, too. She asked if I would be willing to have dinner with the four of them.

"You know," I said to his parents at dinner, "your son is going to die soon. He has some deep-seated anger that is holding him back from expressing his love to you. Don't you think there's a way you can be reconciled to him?"

Sadly, his parents were on another wavelength. They didn't understand me; they thought it was all Steve's problem. After dinner I told Steve's brother-in-law that I didn't see much hope for the parents right now, but that possibly Steve could be persuaded to forgive them. That would be a significant step in itself.

Because of Steve's stern request, his parents had not visited him at the hospital after all. When I went back to see him, I told him I had eaten dinner with them.

"I heard."

We then launched into a lengthy discussion about forgiveness, and how important it is throughout our lives to be able to forgive those who have hurt us—especially our parents—and that sometimes we need to ask forgiveness from those whom we have hurt. At the end of the conversation, he said, "You know, Tom, I think I get it. I've never understood a whole lot about forgiveness, but what you're saying makes a lot of sense to me."

I later found out from Steve's sister that he had written a letter to his parents. "I forgive you for anything you might have done to me as a child," he wrote. "And I hope that you can forgive me and accept me." Even if

Steve never asked Christ into his life, I do believe he had a genuine experience of forgiveness with his parents.

At about that time I got sick myself and went to the hospital for a few days. While I was there, Steve called me and asked how I was doing. I lost touch with him after that.

Though the people I visited often came from similar backgrounds, they responded to me in a variety of ways. One day at St. Vincent's I entered the room of a young black man with AIDS. I could tell by the contortion in his face that he was in a great deal of pain. I said hello, and told him I was a minister. Then I reached out and massaged his foot a little.

As I touched him, he sighed, "Oh, thank you Jesus, thank you Jesus."

"David, do you know Jesus?" I asked.

"Oh, yes . . . yes, I know my Lord," he said, grimacing in pain.

"Well then you know, David, that God is going to take you away from all this suffering, and soon you'll have no more pain."

A smile spread across his face. "I know. I know."

We prayed together. He thanked God for bringing me to him, asked for deliverance from his pain, and prayed for the other AIDS patients in the ward. It was a heartfelt prayer.

Besides visiting hospitals, I also corresponded with a number of people who had written to me—some who had AIDS, others who had a family member with AIDS. Usually I went over to the Fellowship office in the morning to answer mail, and visited patients in the afternoons. In between, I spent a fair amount of time encouraging people by phone, too. (By this time I had left my job in Connecticut and gone on disability.)

I wrote to one man from San Francisco—Bryan—at the request of his sister, who lived in New York. Bryan had been diagnosed with AIDS, but the disease was in its early stages. Around Christmastime he came to visit her, and I met them for dinner.

Bryan and I talked alone for two hours afterward. "I am a believer," he said, "but I am not happy and I am struggling with drugs. I can't get up in the morning without a shot of speed."

His words didn't surprise me. I had already noticed his constricted pupils and hyperactive demeanor, and wondered whether he did drugs. (I knew this from my own experience.)

"Are you high right now?" I asked him.

"Yeah," he answered candidly. "I went into the bathroom just before we started talking and shot up."

Because Bryan was high, I wasn't sure how much of what I said got through to him. He had trouble with Christianity because he didn't agree with its position on homosexuality. He didn't think homosexual behavior was wrong. And he had gotten involved in a church that encouraged homosexual expression.

"You know what, Bryan?" I said. "To be honest, what I'm most worried about right now is your health. Doing drugs on top of having AIDS is going to ruin you even more quickly." I prayed with him, and then he went back to San Francisco.

Some time later I received a nice letter from him. He told me he was trying to give up drugs and that so far he hadn't taken any for four weeks. He also said he was beginning to feel a renewing of his faith, and was experiencing some happiness in his life. I wrote back to him several times, but never heard from him again. His sister reported to me that he was doing very well, however, and that I had helped him.

In the relatively short time that I carried on this ministry, I had a wide variety of opportunities to tell my story and generate greater awareness of the needs of people with AIDS. Sometimes I would accompany B.J.

and speak to retreat groups or churches. I participated in a two-hour Christian radio special on AIDS sponsored by Citihope, a local urban ministry headed by Paul Moore. I taught a four-week seminar on the Christian's response to AIDS at the Lamb's Church. The staff at St. George's Episcopal Church referred parishioners to me who had questions or struggles with homosexuality and AIDS.

Once I gave a five-minute testimony in Carnegie Hall, where Christian musician Steve Green and a well-known black gospel choir from the Brooklyn Tabernacle were performing. I explained that I had AIDS, and told about my conversion experience at Peggy's house and my phone call with Libby afterward. Then I briefly described the huge needs—physical, emotional, and spiritual—of people with AIDS, and challenged the Christian community to get more involved in meeting those needs. When I finished speaking, the entire audience of nearly three thousand people stood up in an overwhelming show of support. I only hoped that their enthusiasm that night would lead to tangible action.

One day my friend Leo called me from the Penn State campus. "You really need to come here, Tom," he said. "There is a large gay rights group here and they need to hear your testimony. They need to hear the Word." I said okay, I would come.

He met me at the tiny train station in State College, Pennsylvania. It was great to see this friend again who had played such an important role in my life. We went out to eat, and then drove to the Student Union building where the meeting was to be held.

On the way there he said, "Tom, I didn't know exactly how to publicize this, so I just put up signs around the campus that said, 'TOM STRIBLING, FORMER HOMO-SEXUAL, WILL GIVE TESTIMONY ON HOW CHRIST CHANGED HIS LIFE.'"

I was nervous, and I didn't know what to expect. The room was filling up as we arrived—probably one hundred-fifty to two hundred students in all. Most of them appeared to be militant gays. They had come to do battle. I'm sure they suspected that I would flatly tell them they were living in sin.

Taking a deep breath, I began my talk, trying my best to be diplomatic, yet not compromising my position. I described my background, and how I had felt homosexual desires since my childhood. I explained how I chose to yield to those desires in college and in graduate school, and how that choice had sent my life into a downward spiral. I told the group that I knew what the gay lifestyle was like, and I understood how powerful the urge was.

But then I went on to tell how I got AIDS, attempted suicide, and eventually came to know God. I said that even though my homosexual orientation had not changed, I believed Christianity taught that the gay lifestyle was contrary to God's will. I concluded by saying how I had a great deal of compassion for homosexuals—especially homosexuals with AIDS—and that I had devoted the rest of my life to bringing them comfort and helping them to experience the love of God.

Thankfully, before the meeting could turn into a name-calling brawl, Leo wrapped everything up at the end. Quite a few students hung around afterward—gay and straight, Christian and non-Christian—and posed questions, which led to more good discussion. Leo and I then went back to my hotel and talked into the wee hours of the morning, catching up on all that had been happening in our lives.

*   *   *

Though by this time my criminal lawsuit had been settled, I had several other legal matters to deal with. My auto insurance company had filed lawsuits against third parties in order to settle claims by Olivia's family, and I had to testify on several occasions. Fortunately, this was all that was left of the personal injury lawsuit that originally had sought ten million dollars in damages. All I could offer, since it was all I had, was the maximum amount of one hundred thousand dollars, payable by my auto insurance company. I learned that it is routine for auto insurance companies to sue as many third parties as they can in order to recover some of their costs. By court order, I was required to cooperate.

A second legal matter weighed more heavily upon me. For some time I had been debating whether to initiate my own lawsuit against my now-former employer, Cooperative Educational Services. I hated the idea of going through the hassle and expense of further litigation, but I hated even more the idea of my employer's getting away with the disgraceful way it had treated me because I had AIDS. (In addition to the strictly job-related hassles, I had also fought with my medical and disability insurance carriers, who had tried to cancel my coverage.)

At first my motive for suing was pure revenge. But as I encountered person after person in the hospital who had experienced similar forms of discrimination, I grew angrier and angrier at the injustice. I realized that employers need to know that they can't get away with these expressions of prejudice. After talking with B.J. and with several lawyers who specialized in discrimination cases, I decided to file a formal suit seeking a financial settlement and back pay. Whatever money we won, if any, would go to support my AIDS ministry.

*   *   *

After my first bout with pneumocystis carinii pneumonia (PCP) in late 1986, when Dr. Grossman had first confirmed my AIDS diagnosis, he told me I probably had one-and-a-half to two years to live. ".That period of time," he said to me, "usually consists of one infection after another. You're in and out of the hospital, and you really don't have any quality of life to speak of." So I had braced myself for another infection.

Instead of getting worse, I had grown stronger. For most of 1987, as I had grown in my newfound faith and laid the groundwork for my ministry, I had had loads of energy. I had gained my weight back to my normal two hundred pounds, and felt great. The PCP had flared up again late that year, but I had wisely gone to the doctor immediately and he had quickly cleared it up with antibiotics.

During this time I had strongly sensed that God wanted me temporarily healthy for a purpose. He had work for me to do, and I had believed he would keep me alive until I had accomplished it. So I had pursued the work of comforting and encouraging people with AIDS. In spite of my good health, however, I had fostered no illusions about my disease—especially after a few hours of visiting AIDS patients at the hospital. Standing next to their beds, I had often felt I was looking at myself, a little further down the road. I had watched many people die, sometimes amid excruciating agony or delirium, and had prayed my death wouldn't replicate theirs. But because I had opened my heart to the love and peace of God, I had no fear of facing eternity.

In 1988 I had experienced only a few setbacks amounting to no more than three weeks total in the hospital. But I could feel my overall energy level declining: I tired more easily, and slept longer. My weight had dropped to one-hundred-eighty pounds. My visitation had continued, but for only three days a week, and I had reduced my traveling considerably.

My health deteriorated more steadily in 1989. Telltale symptoms of the breakdown of my immune system began to occur more frequently: fevers, appetite and energy loss, diarrhea. I lost another twenty pounds. It was difficult for me to manage much more than an occasional hospital visit or speaking engagement. When I wasn't sick, I'd stop in at the Fellowship several mornings each week to check the mail and have lunch with B.J. if he was in. Afternoons were spent at home resting, catching up on correspondence, or talking on the phone with family, friends, and AIDS patients I'd visited.

I realized that my focus was beginning to shift from visiting other patients to being one myself. As I grew weaker, I knew that I could only do so much for others. My time would be up soon. Now I needed to turn to the people around me—my family, my daughter Libby, B.J., my friends—and allow them to support me the way I had tried to support others.

*P*raise be to the God and Father of our Lord Jesus Christ, the Father of compassion and the God of all comfort, who comforts us in all our troubles, so that we can comfort those in any trouble with the comfort we ourselves have received from God. For just as the sufferings of Christ flow over into our lives, so also through Christ our comfort overflows (2 Corinthians 1:3–5).

ELEVEN
ELEVEN
ELEVEN
ELEVEN
ELEVEN

"What can I do to help people with AIDS? What do they really need?"

I have been asked these questions many times since beginning my ministry. There are a number of ways to answer. I would start by saying that people with AIDS—particularly in the advanced stages—need virtually all the same things that any terminally ill person would need. They are in and out of the hospital frequently, and eventually stay there for longer and longer periods of time.

When they're in the hospital, they need visitors: people who will stop in regularly, who will hold their hand, who will bring a cheery greeting card or photo to stick on the wall—people who will talk sometimes, and just sit quietly and be there at other times. They also need one or two special people to mind their affairs back home: make sure the house is secure, feed the cat and the goldfish, water the plants, go through the mail and handle anything important (with their consent, of course), check the answering machine for phone messages, toss out moldy items from the refrigerator, vacuum, dust, and so on.

When they're home, they're often too weak to do much other than rest. They need friends to run errands such as grocery shopping. They may need rides to doctor's appointments or to church. They greatly appreciate people who arrange to drop off a warm dinner, even if they're not able to stay and share it. And they probably still need help with household chores such as laundry and the dishes.

AIDS patients, just like cancer patients or anyone with a terminal illness, need these practical, everyday kinds of help. But what kinds of needs are *unique* to people with AIDS? What do they need most?

First, they need their family and friends to stand by them.

Think about it: When someone gets cancer, family, friends, and the church tend to *rally around* the sick person, providing all kinds of support. But when a person gets AIDS, people tend to *abandon* the sufferer—at the very time they are needed most. Many parents are unwilling even to *admit* that their son or daughter has AIDS, much less to actually visit and care for him or her. There's a strong embarrassment and shame factor at work, even in non-Christian families. Homosexual promiscuity and intravenous drug use—the two primary ways to contract AIDS—are not considered acceptable behavior by our society in general. When people contract the disease, then, those around them tend to say they deserve it, and offer little or no support.

Some Christians take this idea a step further, proclaiming that AIDS is a sign of God's judgment on homosexuals. What a sad and uninformed position to take. Yes, the Bible clearly states that homosexual behavior is sinful. Yes, sinful actions can have negative consequences. But God doesn't *kill* people who cheat, lie, steal, gossip, or commit adultery. What would make him decide to kill homosexuals?

Furthermore, homosexuals aren't the only people coming down with AIDS. What about those who have picked up the AIDS virus through a blood transfusion? What about the innocent wives of bisexual men who were never told about their husband's "other" life? What about the babies of AIDS-carrying women who will be born with AIDS? Is it God's plan to kill them, too?

What Christians and others need to do about AIDS patients is to quit judging them and start loving them.

For this reason I feel somewhat suspicious of a church program to "evangelize" people with AIDS: the implication seems to be that if they become Christians, then they'll somehow "qualify" for the church's support. I desire with all my heart that people with AIDS who don't know Christ come to know him. But I think they'll be more likely to do so if the church's primary motive is providing Christian love and comfort rather than evangelism.

People with AIDS need to feel supported by a caring, nurturing community of friends. They need more than occasional visitors and errand runners and hit-and-run evangelists: they need a support network of loving people who will listen and talk, pray and play, laugh and cry with them. Right up to the end. It's a lot to ask, but it's what they really need.

Second, they need housing.

As I spent time with AIDS patients and got to know them better, I realized that many of them had no home to return to when they got out of the hospital. There were a variety of reasons for this. Some had lost their jobs (or, like me, had been demoted) when their employer discovered they had AIDS. Unable to pay their rent, they were evicted by their landlords. Others had been thrown out by roommates, or disowned by their families. As a result, many were forced to stay in the hospital for months simply because they had no other place to go.

(Closely related to the housing need is the need for legal advocacy, so that people with AIDS can successfully fight discrimination by landlords and employers. At present, an organization known as the Gay Men's Health Crisis provides the best help in New York along these lines. What a powerful witness it would be for Christians to get involved in this kind of work.)

I began to wonder what could be done about the housing problem. Would it be possible to buy a home or an apartment building and convert it into a hospice-type setting for people with AIDS? Could a group of local churches combine efforts to provide funding and volunteers to run such a place? I drew up a plan, and B.J. and I took it around to various churches in New York City. At first they expressed strong interest in the program; but then, one by one, for various reasons, they backed out.

The need remains, however. Some big cities have opened AIDS hospices, but they are few and far between, and seldom church-sponsored. (In New York, for instance, Trinity Episcopal Church helps to sponsor Bailey House, a former hotel that has been converted into housing for about sixty men and women with AIDS.) Here is a huge opportunity for the church to get involved at the practical level in the lives of people with AIDS. It would take a great deal of commitment, and would probably require several churches to work together, but I believe it could be done.

What I envision is a Christian community—a large house with four or five bedrooms, or a cluster of apartments. AIDS patients would move in while they were still mobile and able to take care of themselves. Perhaps a "housemother" would come each day and take care of the cooking, cleaning, and laundry. A time of prayer and celebration of the Eucharist would take place each day, though I would not require all residents to be Christians. The purpose would be to provide a caring, supportive, Christian environment where AIDS patients can love each other and experience the love of God and of the church.

As residents become increasingly ill, home nursing care would be provided, and other residents and people from the church would gather around them, sit with them, and love them until they die.

I haven't seen anything like this happen yet, but I believe that one day, after I'm gone, it will happen.

*   *   *

The clatter of construction continues outside my apartment window. I glance over to my desk, where the phone remains silent.

On a shelf above the phone stands a cluster of photos of my family and friends—the people I've shared so much joy and pain with. It occurs to me that these people and many others have indeed given me all the kinds of support I've described above. Not a day goes by without someone calling or stopping by to say hello. My ever-present, ever-caring sister, Peggy, calls nearly every day, as do my parents. Jerry and my father have flown in several times from the Midwest (my mother has been ill with Parkinson's), and I've traveled to see them, too. B.J. and others from the Fellowship carve out time for me, and Father William has written me some wonderful letters. The Lamb's Church has so kindly provided me with this apartment, welcomed me into their congregation, and assisted me with errands and meals. Even Andrew and Tony and Will have kept in touch. God has richly blessed me through all of these people. I hope that I'll be conscious of their presence and be able to talk to them—right up to the end.

In one of the pictures on my shelf, I am walking with Libby on a sunny city street, my arm around her shoulder. Now twenty-three, she frequently comes down from Boston for the weekend. She knows my time is short, and tries to visit whenever she can. With all that has happened in our lives and all the years we spent apart, it sometimes feels as if we're just getting to know one another. I must be something of a mystery to her, this man who was a homosexual, a minister, and her father. This man who

193

always adored her, but who abandoned her for a lifestyle of emptiness. And now, this man whose spirit has been awakened by the love of God, and whose soul will soon enter his presence.

I am unshakably convinced that God has forgiven my sins, that there is a heaven, and that I'll be going there. "Libby, I'm not afraid to die," I told her once when she visited me at the hospital. "I'm not afraid, because I know where I'm going. I'm ready." She cried when I said that. Dying is a frightening thing, especially if one is not at peace with God. But Libby is strong, and deep down she knows that I've found that peace. I only hope she'll recognize how much her unwavering love for me helped to undo my heart.

The ringing of the telephone interrupts my thoughts. It's the doctor. He wants me back in the hospital.

*B*arring some miracle, I will most certainly die. And I will suffer the pain of saying good-bye, of watching my body waste away. But I have a new way of understanding death and a new appreciation of the real value of this fleshly body. As those who loved me back from death to new life gather around me to support me in my hour of death, I want there to be a sense of celebration.

But, though dying, I am at the same time more alive than I was before I was diagnosed with this terminal illness. I see life with new eyes, and I believe that it has a purpose and meaning far beyond our ability to fully comprehend. That purpose continues, just as life does, far beyond this mortal sphere.

From a sermon Tom preached, 1988

EPILOGUE
EPILOGUE
EPILOGUE
EPILOGUE
EPILOGUE

In a small, stark hospital room at the New York University Medical Center in Manhattan, a man lay dying of AIDS. The disease had ravaged his body so completely that he looked like a heap of bones with waxy, blotchy skin stretched over them. He lay in a semi-fetal position, mainly to keep warm, since he had no fat to maintain his body temperature. Posted outside the door was a sign that said in large, bold letters: BIOCHEMICAL HAZARD. Whenever nurses entered the room, they wore rubber gloves. When they left, they tossed the gloves in a special, covered bin labeled BIOCHEMICAL WASTE.

The man's name was Tom Stribling. In response to his doctor's phone call, he had admitted himself on June 10. Two-and-a-half months later, he still hadn't left. Numerous tests and several surgeries had left his already-failing body even weaker. There were a few good days, a few encouraging days, and many painful and uncomfortable ones. Brad Noffsinger, B.J.'s assistant at the Fellowship, watched Tom's apartment and handled many of his personal matters. Libby, Jerry, Peggy, Tom's father, B.J., and others visited him, held his hand, offered comfort, told him how much he was loved.

Thankfully, Tom retained his mental faculties during these months. At the end of August, knowing that he had very little time, he made a final request: to spend his remaining days in Cedar Rapids, Iowa, with Peggy and her family. Cedar Rapids, where only two-and-a-half years ago Tom had felt such an outpouring of love from his sister and her family, from his parents, from his daughter. Where God had reached down through a little hole in heaven and opened Tom's heart.

Before he left New York, Barry Abell came to say good-bye. Barry, a former college football player and now executive vice-president of the bonds division of a Wall Street brokerage firm, had attended the same Bible study as Tom. Initially he'd been afraid of Tom's disease, but in a short time he realized he had nothing to be afraid of, and had grown to love and respect Tom greatly.

"I want to ask you one last question," he said to Tom. "It's kind of personal. Does it work, Tom? I mean, does this whole thing with Jesus and Christianity really work? With all the pain and suffering you've gone through, do you still have the peace of Christ?"

Though Tom was now very weak and found it difficult to talk, his face immediately brightened.

He turned to him and said, "Yes, Barry, it does. It really does work. And yes, I am at peace with Jesus."

Afterward, as Barry told B.J. about his conversation, he said, "I used to be afraid to even shake his hand, and there I was, hugging and kissing him good-bye."

Knowing that he probably wouldn't see Tom again, B.J. said his own tearful good-bye in New York.

"What are you crying for, Beej?" Tom broke in. "It's going to be okay. I'm going to be with the Lord. Isn't that what this is all about?"

Tom arrived safely in Iowa. And on September 6, 1989, with Peggy and his parents at his side, Tom took the last breath of Cedar Rapids air his diseased body could hold. A moment later, he stood in the presence of his heavenly Father, alive and whole.

RESOURCES

General AIDS information:

AIDS
P.O. Box 14252
Washington, DC 20044
301-443-0292
(For a free copy of the Surgeon General's Report on AIDS)

AIDS Crisis & Christians Today (ACCT)
P.O. Box 24647
Nashville, TN 37202-4647
615-371-1616

AIDS Information Line
(U.S. Department of Health and Human Services)
800-342-AIDS

American Red Cross
National AIDS Education Program
1730 D Street, N.W.
Washington, DC 20006
202-639-3223

Americans for a Sound AIDS Policy
P.O. Box 17433

Washington, DC 20041
703-471-7350

National AIDS Information Clearing House
(Centers for Disease Control)
P.O. Box 6003
Rockville, MD 20850
800-458-5231
301-762-5111

National Hospice Organization
1901 N. Moore Street
Arlington, VA 22209
703-243-5900

Victory House
719 S.W. 4th Court
Ft. Lauderdale, FL 33312
305-463-0848
(For locations of Christian AIDS hospices or live-in
facilities)